Mesopotamian
Myths

Acknowledgements

I am most grateful to Dr S. M. Dalley of Oxford University for her kind and helpful criticisms of the text, and to Dr Roger Moorey of the Ashmolean Museum and Christopher Walker, Dr Dominique Collon and Judy Rudoe of the British Museum for their help with the illustrations. I also thank my husband Christopher for his continuing help and support.

THE · LEGENDARY · PAST

Mesopotamian Myths

HENRIETTA McCALL

Published in cooperation with
BRITISH MUSEUM PUBLICATIONS
UNIVERSITY OF TEXAS PRESS, AUSTIN

International Standard Book Number 0–292–75130–3
Library of Congress Catalog Card Number 90–83365

Printed in Great Britain by The Bath Press, Avon

Second University of Texas Press printing, 1993

Requests for permission to reproduce material
from this work should be sent to Permissions,
University of Texas Press, Box 7819, Austin,
Texas 78713–7819

Designed by Gill Mouqué
Cover design by Slatter-Anderson

FRONT COVER *Detail suggestive of the Flood
story, from a palace fresco of King Zimri-Lim
of Mari (eighteenth century BC).*

THIS PAGE *View of the Iraqi marshes.*

Author's Note

Where possible, the Akkadian text has been
reinforced using fragments and duplicates,
but many gaps still remain. Parallel
passages sometimes allow them to be filled,
and square brackets [ ] indicate where such
words have been inserted. Where this has
not been possible, missing words and
phrases are noted by . . . and untranslatable
terms are rendered as transliterations in
italics.

Contents

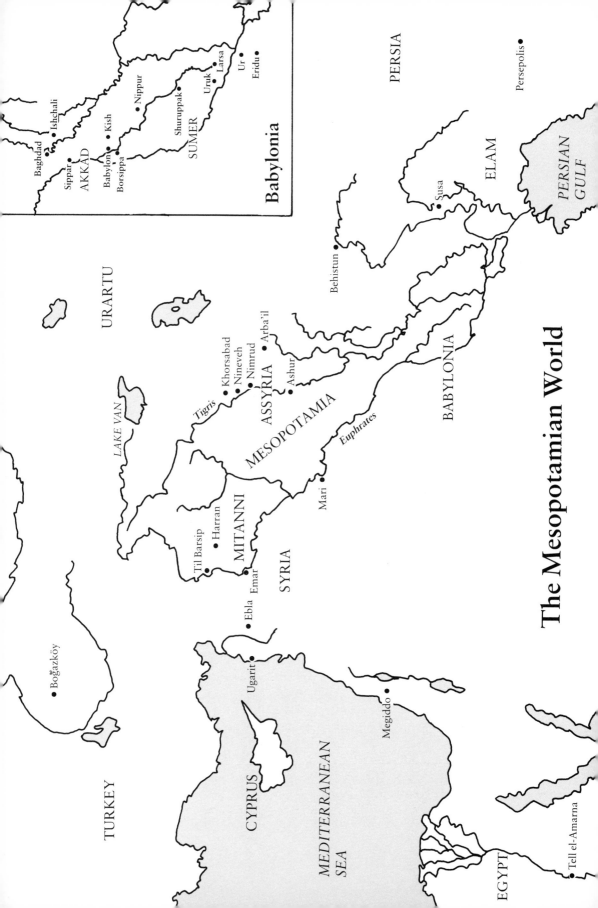

The Mesopotamian World

Babylonia (inset map)

Baghdad
Ishchali
Sippar
AKKAD
Babylon • Kish
Borsippa
Nippur
Shuruppak
SUMER
Uruk
Larsa
Ur • Eridu

TURKEY

URARTU

LAKE VAN

Boğazköy

CYPRUS

MEDITERRANEAN
SEA

Ugarit •

Ebla • Emar •

Til Barsip • Harran
MITANNI

SYRIA

Megiddo •

EGYPT

Tell el-Amarna •

Khorsabad
Nineveh • Arba'il
Nimrud
ASSYRIA • Ashur

Tigris

MESOPOTAMIA

Euphrates

Mari •

BABYLONIA

Behistun •

PERSIA

Persepolis •

ELAM

Susa •

PERSIAN
GULF

Introduction

Mesopotamia, that ancient land comprising Assyria in the north and Babylonia in the south, is to many unfamiliar territory. Some aspects are of course well known from its biblical connections: the glories of Nineveh and Babylon, the bloodthirsty nature of the Assyrian warriors, the magical power of the Babylonian diviners, the rich and powerful merchants, the luxurious and sensual lifestyle. The names of Hammurabi, Nebuchadrezzar, Tiglath-Pileser, Ashurbanipal and Sennacherib are potent ones. The mighty reliefs in the British Museum and the Louvre tell of victory, order, authority; they show battle preparations, fighting, sieges, chariots and splendid lion hunts. As befits the sheer size of these reliefs, their guardians are truly monumental: colossal winged bulls and lions, five-legged and immaculately curled and harnessed. Much of what we know of those ancient civilisations is what those who lived there so long ago wanted us to know. It is propaganda on a grand scale.

But it is quite another matter when it comes to records that were not deliberately meant to speak to posterity. Mesopotamia has yielded vast collections of clay tablets which record everything from the simplest sheep count to the most arcane divination procedure. These make up a corpus representing matters of current interest amongst the people of their day. Such things are not easy to digest or to interpret in a world far removed from their origins. For that reason perhaps they are of all the greater interest.

Though much of the information in these tablets may be thought of as mundane, they include amongst them a small proportion of tablets which can properly be described as literary. In them are told stories which are for the most part still unfamiliar, though in antiquity some at least were well known. These stories survived unread from about the time of the birth of Christ until halfway through the last century when Akkadian, the language in which they were written, was first deciphered. The story of their decipherment and impact is told in the first chapter of this book.

In the longest myth, the **Epic of Gilgamesh**, the hero Gilgamesh is a semi-divine king of Uruk, who, after the death of his friend Enkidu, goes in search of eternal life, a quest which takes him to Ut-napishtim, the survivor of a great flood. A flood sent to punish mankind is also a theme in the myth of **Atrahasis**. The **Epic of Creation** tells of the world's beginnings and of the building of the great city of Babylon under the protection of its god Marduk. Shorter myths are the **Descent of Ishtar to the Underworld**, in which the goddess Ishtar goes down to visit her sister Ereshkigal, the queen of the underworld, and almost fails to return. A similar myth in many respects is that of **Nergal and Ereshkigal**, in which Nergal descends to the land of no return and seduces its queen. The **Epic of Erra** tells of Babylon in decline, its patron god temporarily absent; **Etana**, of a childless king in search of a magical plant that will ensure him an heir; **Adapa**, of a priest of Ea who deliberately breaks the wing of South Wind and is taken to heaven to answer for his behaviour; and the **Epic of Anzu** relates the story of a wicked bird who snatches from the god Ellil the Tablet of Destinies (which bestowed supreme power on the one who held it), and is slain in glorious combat by the god Ninurta.

All the myths concern the gods and people of Mesopotamia, most of whom behaved – well or badly – in a way that was reassuringly familiar to their audience. The more exciting and unpredictable parts of these myths tend to occur in locations which would have been extraordinary, but real enough to command attention: in forests, by the sea, in the mountains. The pace of the action is always slow moving, and quite often presaged by dreams and warnings or even described in advance by another character, so there are few surprises and little suspense. Fixed epithets abound, which increase the stately character of the texts.

The translations given in this book preserve the lengths and order of the lines on the tablets. Rhyming verse as we would define it is not apparent, but literary devices such as puns, alliteration and onomatopoeia all help to create internal rhythms.

The way in which sequential ordering is used, and the device whereby an action is repeated once, twice, a third time, and so on, in order to heighten dramatic tension, has been maintained in the excerpts given here. In the same spirit, the temptation for the translator to use several different adjectives when the Akkadian limits itself to one, or to embroider the text for a more sophisticated modern audience, has been avoided. The translations reflect, as far as is possible, the rock-hard impact and subtle qualities inherent in the originals.

I am deeply indebted to Dr S. M. Dalley of Oxford University for the translations, which have been taken from her book *Myths from Mesopotamia* (Oxford, 1989).

Discovery and decipherment

In the first half of the seventeenth century, an urbane and well-educated Italian nobleman called Pietro della Valle made a spectacular journey to the east, a journey which began in Venice and took him to Constantinople, Alexandria, over the Sinai desert, back to the pyramids, across Palestine by caravan, to Damascus, Aleppo and Baghdad. There he married a beautiful Nestorian Christian and a year later set off once more with his bride. They went to Isfahan and Persepolis, the capital city of the Achaemenid Dynasty of Persia (559–331 BC), the glories of which della Valle was one of the earliest travellers to describe. He also copied a number of inscriptions carved on the palace doors in three different versions of a strange wedge-shaped script.

Twelve years later he returned to his native Rome, having visited India en route. His wife had died some ten years earlier and her embalmed body had accompanied him ever since. Also with him were his copies of the inscriptions from Persepolis. It was the first sight in the West of that exotic cryptic script.

In 1700 the Regius Professor of Hebrew at Oxford, Thomas Hyde, wrote about della Valle's acquisitions in a paper entitled 'Dactuli pyramidales seu cuneiformes' (signs of pyramidal or wedge-shape), and it was as cuneiform that this wedge-shaped script came to be known. Decipherment, however, lay some time in the future.

The German Georg Friedrich Grotefend realised that the three versions of della Valle's Persepolitan inscription represented three separate languages: Old Persian, Elamite and Babylonian, none of which was understood. Grotefend decided to begin with the Old Persian version and by 1802 was able to present a convincing transliteration. Meanwhile, scholars in France, Germany and Denmark were also working on the same inscription, a further copy of which had been made by a Dane, Carsten Niebuhr, and published in 1772.

It was, however, an Englishman, Henry Creswicke Rawlinson, who was the first to present a convincing translation of an Old Persian inscription in a paper he read to the Royal Asiatic Society in London in 1838. Only three years earlier he had, according to an autobiographical note, begun 'the study of the cuneiform inscriptions of Persia, being then stationed at Kermanshah ...'. During 1835 and 1836 Rawlinson had copied the Old Persian part of a trilingual inscription carved high on the side of a mountain at Behistun (Bisitun) in western Iran. In 1844 he scaled the same mountainside again to tackle the Babylonian part of it. It took him three years: with the help of an agile local boy he was winched up the perpendicular rock-face by means of ropes and ladders and then hung precariously 300 ft (100 m) above ground, first cleaning the inscriptions and then copying them. Within two years he had correctly deciphered 246 individual signs of an approximate total of 600. His pioneering work was published by the Royal Asiatic Society in 1852.

Meanwhile, interest in Assyrian matters was growing in Europe. In March 1843 Paul Emile Botta had begun to excavate at Khorsabad, built by Sargon II at the end of the eighth century BC to be his new capital. Almost immediately Botta began to uncover limestone slabs sculptured in relief. In 1845 Austen Henry Layard began digging at Nimrud, biblical Calah, built as his new capital by Ashurnasirpal II in 879 BC. Almost straightaway, Layard too struck treasure: immense stone panels inscribed with horses and riders, abject captives, sieges, attacks on fortified cities, warriors fording rivers, archers on chariots. There were also scenes of lion hunts, and a strange anthropomorphic image of an hawk-headed deity, 7 ft (over 2 m) high. Some of the panels were additionally inscribed with cuneiform. In 1846 Layard was joined by an assistant, Hormuzd Rassam, brother of the British vice-consul at Mosul. Together they uncovered large fragments of colossal winged bull-men, and yet more inscribed stone panels. A large collection of these objects, including the Black Obelisk of Shalmaneser III, were sent – not without difficulty because of their bulk and weight – to the British Museum. Meanwhile, Botta's finds had found their cumbersome way to Paris.

In June 1847, when the colossi and great reliefs arrived in London, it was by no means certain how the public would react. What interest there was in the Assyrians was based on their bad reputation, fostered by the Bible

Pietro della Valle

Henry Creswicke Rawlinson

Drawing (above left) showing the tripartite cuneiform inscription high on the cliff side at Behistun; (right) the Black Obelisk of Shalmaneser III.

and by classical authors and scholars. The Assyrians were seen not only as vain and violent marauders intent on rape and pillage, but also as loose, debauched and immoral in their home life. This was hardly likely to appeal to the Victorian public. But in fact they found the exhibition very much to their taste, the sheer size and confident execution of the objects suggesting another much earlier empire based on the same unshakeable faith in its own enduring permanence. The public flocked to the British Museum, encouraged by *The Illustrated London News* with a full-page spread and several fine line illustrations: 'The recent excavations and discoveries' would excite the curiosity 'not only of the antiquarian but of all scriptural students, from the illustration which they afford of passages in Holy Writ ...'; the magazine went on to give a minute description of the eleven panels. In late August there was a second arrival of some fifteen further items. *The Illustrated London News* made the comment, despite five further line drawings which rather belied it, that 'this second collection of sculptures is deficient in that poetical and historical interest which so eminently distinguished the previous arrival

...'. In 1849 Layard published *Nineveh & Its Remains*, his own account of the excavations, and in its first year the book sold eight thousand copies, which would, according to Layard, 'place it side by side with Mrs Rundell's Cookery'.

In 1851, at the time of the Great Exhibition, Assyrian revival was in full flood. Jewellery was made displaying motifs from the huge stone tablets, and the London firm of Henry Wilkinson & Co. produced electroplated wine coolers engraved with human-headed bulls and an Assyrian king. The winged bull or lion on a bracket became a fairly common architectural feature both in England and France. A 'winged bull from Nineveh' made an appearance

Silver gilt casket (above) presented to Austen Henry Layard in 1853. The front shows a scene of King Ashurbanipal lion-hunting, with a winged bull to the left and a winged lion to the right.

Gold and enamel bracelet (below) in the Assyrian revival style. Made in London about 1872.

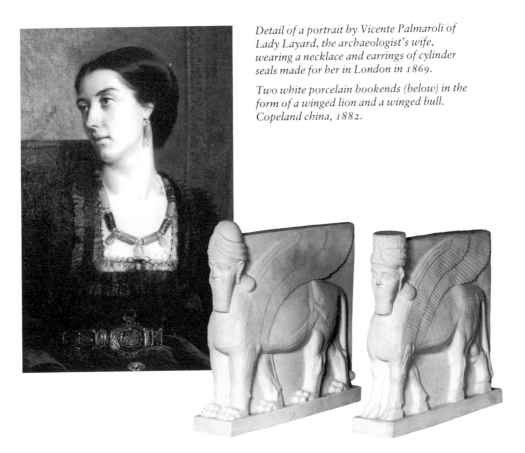

Detail of a portrait by Vicente Palmaroli of Lady Layard, the archaeologist's wife, wearing a necklace and earrings of cylinder seals made for her in London in 1869.

Two white porcelain bookends (below) in the form of a winged lion and a winged bull. Copeland china, 1882.

in a popular song and, in 1880, Maj.-Gen. Rawlinson himself was gently lampooned by Gilbert and Sullivan: in *The Pirates of Penzance* the modern major-general sang, 'I can write a washing-bill in Babylonic cuneiform'.

Thus, by the time Rawlinson published his Behistun inscription in 1852, some familiarity already existed together with a growing interest in the ancient Assyrian civilisation. In 1853 the Assyrian Excavation Fund was founded and sponsored W. K. Loftus to excavate at Warka, ancient Uruk. But it was not until twenty years later that the new skill of reading cuneiform tablets at last made it possible for scholars to try interpreting this ancient civilisation.

George Smith was only seven years old when the first objects from ancient Mesopotamia arrived at the British Museum. He was born in 1840 and received little formal education before being apprenticed into the trade of bank-note engraving. Early on, however, he became fascinated by Assyriology and before he was twenty had become such a familiar figure at the British Museum that no less a personage than Henry Rawlinson himself took an interest in him, allowing the young man to use his own room, where he could work on clay tablets. Such was the calibre of his work that, in 1867, Smith was appointed an assistant in the Assyriology section of the Museum, and in 1871 he published *Annals of Assurbanipal*.

Smith had also been busy cataloguing the collection of tablets in the Assyriology section according to subject matter. Into the compartment labelled 'Mythological and Mythical' he put together some eighty tablets from the library of Ashurbanipal at Nineveh, and when he had collated one of them and begun to translate, he suddenly realised he was reading the familiar story of the Flood. He was so overcome with excitement that he rushed around the room and began tearing off his clothes.

Some months later on 3 December 1872 he read a paper to the Society of Biblical Archaeology. His announcement caused a flurry of excitement: a heathen text, apparently anticipating Noah's Ark. His audience was all agog.

The owner of the *Daily Telegraph*, Sir Edwin Arnold, offered the British Museum a thousand guineas to allow Smith himself to go to Nineveh in search of the rest of the tablet. Smith set out in January 1873, but it was not until the beginning of May that the necessary formalities were agreed with the Ottoman governor in Mosul. Once Smith began work, turning over the debris of previous excavations and searching out fragments of inscribed material, he was almost immediately rewarded. It was his custom to spend his evenings going over the day's finds and, on the fifth evening, he found to his 'surprise and gratification' that one of the fragments he had just wiped clean contained the best part of seventeen missing lines apparently belonging to the first column of the Flood tablet and 'fitting into the only place where there was a blank in the story' of Gilgamesh.

Later that year Smith returned once more to Nineveh. As he later recounted in a letter to the *Daily Telegraph* (4 March 1875), he had taken home with him from his first expedition another interesting fragment, apparently unrelated to the Epic of Gilgamesh. When he found time to look closely at it, he realised with mounting excitement that this one was 'part of the Chaldean story of the Creation', and he determined to find as much of the rest as he could. On his second expedition, by a similar stroke of luck, he discovered in the debris where he had found the missing fragment of Tablet XI of Gilgamesh 'another portion belonging to this story, far more precious ... This turns out to contain the story of man's original innocence, of the temptation, and of the fall'.

Smith had stumbled upon fragments of another myth which we now call the Epic of Creation. Piecing these together in the British Museum, he was able to draw parallels with the biblical account of man's creation in Genesis. He promised the readers of the *Daily Telegraph* that 'when my investigations are completed I will publish a full account and translation of these Genesis legends, all of which I have now been fortunate to find ...'

Unfortunately, Smith was unable to fulfil his promise. On his third expedition to Nineveh he contracted a virulent strain of fever and died in Aleppo on 19 August 1876, aged thirty-six.

The interest aroused by his work did not die with him. In 1885 O. C. Whitehouse published an English translation of Eberhard Schrader's popular

George Smith

Professor Doctor Friedrich Delitzsch

work *Die Keilinschriften und das alte Testament* (*The Cuneiform Inscriptions and the Old Testament*), which went into a second edition in 1888. Schrader's original work went into three editions, and in 1903 was entirely rewritten by H. Zimmern and H. Winckler. The latter then published his own book on those cuneiform inscriptions which illustrated biblical material.

In Germany a storm of controversy arose when the leading figure in Assyriology of the time, Friedrich Delitzsch, delivered a lecture entitled 'Babel und Bibel' on 13 January 1902 to the German Oriental Society, whose audience included Kaiser Wilhelm II. This lecture became an historic event. Delitzsch's new and exact translations showed that the Bible was not, as previously thought, the world's oldest book but was in fact preceded by literature from a much earlier epoch. There were great similarities between the two ancient worlds, but the Old Testament could in his view no longer be regarded as unique and therefore as pure revelation. In fact, Delitzsch's work questioned the fundamental authority of the Old Testament. Such was the outrage at the first lecture that a year later Delitzsch gave a second, urging theologians to take a balanced view in dealing with what they saw as attacks on cherished portions of the Bible, and to make provision for the teaching of Assyriology: 'There is no need to swallow everything whole, nor to toss the Bible on the shelf as antiquated rubbish'.

This was not enough for the Kaiser who, perhaps wishing to disassociate himself from his earlier enthusiasm, wrote to the weekly review *Grenzboten* on 19 February 1903 describing it as 'a great mistake' that Professor Delitzsch should have approached the question of revelation in such a 'very polemical spirit'. 'Religion', he wrote, 'has never been the result of science, but the outpouring of the heart and being of man from his intercourse with God.'

A week later *The Times* in London printed a long defence of Delitzsch by his 'friend and fellow worker in the field of Assyrian research for more than twenty-five years', W. St Chad Boscawen, who said Delitzsch was the victim of an imperial attack strong enough to unseat him from his chair at Berlin University because, as a 'mere historian and Assyriologist', he had 'dared to enter the world of theological and religious conclusions and hypotheses'.

Less controversial was a work of translation published in 1909, which became the standard reference for biblical scholars. This was Hugo Gressmann's *Altorientalische Texte und Bilde zum alten Testament* ('Old Oriental texts and images of the Old Testament'). Less than twenty years later, in 1926, an entirely new edition was necessary because of discoveries of new texts and improved understanding of old ones. The quantity of translations presented to readers had almost doubled.

The first English collection of cuneiform texts, *Cuneiform Parallels in the Old Testament*, was published by R. W. Rogers in 1912. The available material was given both in transliteration and in translation. This was followed in 1916 by G. A. Barton's *Archaeology and the Bible*, which contained translations interspersed with notes drawing attention to biblical parallels. This book was periodically revised; a seventh edition appeared in 1937. A further major landmark was the publication in 1950 of *Ancient Near Eastern Texts* by the Princeton University Press, almost exactly a century after Rawlinson published his Behistun inscription. This large collection of texts was chosen on the basis that they were parallels to, or illustrative of, certain passages in the Old Testament. Criteria for inclusion were the appearance of a biblical name, the treatment of a biblical theme, or that the text represented a type of literary form (such as a prayer, lamentation or ritual) prominently featured in the Old Testament.

From this it can be seen that for a long time the overriding interest in texts from Mesopotamia was in their biblical connection. Throughout the nineteenth century, authentication of the Bible had been a major preoccupation among the reading classes. This preoccupation became paramount halfway through the century, when scientific progress began to compete with religious belief. Darwin's *Origin of Species*, supported by pioneer work in dating fossils, proved that the earth was millions rather than thousands of years old, and that life had evolved over that long period and had not been created in a single week. This made people question for the first time the literal truth of the Bible. And they found such questioning very disturbing. At the same time, they wanted 'proof' or otherwise of such events as Noah's Flood. It was not surprising, therefore, that the newly legible myths from Mesopotamia which seemed to offer that proof made such an impact when they first came to public attention. Nowadays they are considered in their own right as a literary corpus with its own independent merits. There will always be an argument, however, for comparison with Old Testament texts, not only for the light this can shed on the Bible, but also because such a comparison provides a unique opportunity for observing Mesopotamia from the outside.

Definitions and literary tradition

Collecting together the myths available to us today was the work of many decades. Luck, fate and chance, as well as the more scientific approach to excavation adopted in recent years, have all played their part. The table overleaf summarises such information as we have for each of the myths which make up the main corpus of Babylonian literature. Because the available material is patchy and we need to rely to a great extent on our own applied criteria, particularly in trying to assess the time of a composition, the information provided must inevitably be somewhat uneven, and we must be prepared to leave some blanks. Otherwise we run the risk of assuming too much and drawing false conclusions. Perhaps further research and discovery will enable some of the blanks to be filled in.

A glance at the table will reveal how often the place of discovery is Nineveh. The royal libraries uncovered there have indeed provided much of the material available to us, some of it in the best preserved condition, but Nineveh was only one of the many sites all over Mesopotamia where libraries and archives existed. Excavation almost anywhere will turn up at least a few tablets, even if they only record numbers of cattle and household lists. Collections of tablets were made at all periods and their remains have been found in Ashur and Harran in the north and Babylon, Ur, Nippur, Uruk and Borsippa in the south.

The existence of these collections is to some extent the result of the way scribes were trained; this remained virtually unchanged for two millennia. It included the faithful copying of texts over and over again. Scribes throughout the country probably became the owners of the texts they had copied during their apprenticeship and thus practically identical copies of texts were taken to different locations. We should distinguish, however, between collections of school exercises such as those found at Sultantepe (complete with some schoolboy howlers); administrative archives, such as those found *in situ* at Ebla and scattered at Mari; and a 'true' library, that is a deliberate collection of fine literature brought together for the motive of collection itself, probably in a palace or temple.

We should also be aware that, although the durability of clay tablets and their widespread distribution patterns may be good news for modern scholars, haphazard discovery, inept excavation methods and the occasional use of more ephemeral wax-covered wooden boards are less so. Some very popular texts may never have been found at all, and we may be misled into

Evidence of the Myths

MYTH	NUMBER OF TABLETS / APPROXIMATE LINE LENGTH		CHIEF LOCATIONS OF DISCOVERY IN MESOPOTAMIA
Epic of Gilgamesh	12 tablets		Ur, Sippar, Ishchali ←
	3000 lines		Nineveh (Libraries of Sennacherib and Ashurbanipal)
Epic of Creation	7 tablets		Nineveh ←
			Ashur, Kish
	1000 lines		Sultantepe ←
Epic of Erra	originally 5 tablets (two-thirds preserved)		Assyria: Nineveh, Ashur, Sultantepe
	c. 750 lines		Babylonia: Babylon, Ur, Tell Haddad
Etana	substantial fragments only		Ashur ←
	originally c.450 lines		Nineveh ←
Adapa			
	c.120 lines		Nineveh ←
Anzu	3 tablets		Tarbiṣu, Sultantepe
	720 lines		Nineveh
Descent of Ishtar			Ashur ←
	150 lines		Nineveh ←
Nergal and Ereshkigal			Sultantepe ←
	750 lines		
Atrahasis	3 tablets		Sippar ←
	originally 1245 lines		Nineveh ←

NOTE: Times of composition are not necessarily analogous to chief locations of discovery; some tablets uncovered at the main sites (particularly royal libraries) were copies of much earlier texts. Arrows pointing from times of composition relate to specific location(s).

TIMES OF COMPOSITION	OTHER LOCATIONS OF DISCOVERY	OTHER VERSIONS
—— Old Babylonian period (5 tablets), early 2nd millennium BC	Boğazköy, Megiddo, Ugarit, Emar, Elam	Early Sumerian c. 2150 BC Also translations into Hittite, Hurrian, Elamite
—— Old Babylonian period? —— 7th century BC		
c. 9th–7th century BC		
Old Babylonian period ———→ Susa —— Middle Assyrian, 13th century BC —— Neo-Assyrian, mid 1st millennium BC		
15th, 14th century BC ———→ Tell-el-Amarna —— late 2nd millennium BC		
Old Babylonian period; Standard Babylonian, 7th century BC	Susa	Sumerian; story probably familiar to Hurrians
—— end 2nd millennium BC —— 7th century BC		Earlier and longer (410 lines) Sumerian version: Descent of Inanna
15th century BC ———→ Tell el-Amarna (shorter version: 90 lines) —— 7th century BC		
—— Old Babylonian period, probably before 1645 BC —— 8th–7th century BC		

The Epic of Gilgamesh: Tablet XI, the 'Flood Tablet'.

believing that some texts were more popular in antiquity than they actually were, just because so many fragments of these have come to light.

How representative of the literary tradition as a whole is the literature which has survived? Royal libraries, in particular that of Ashurbanipal in Nineveh, provide one of the best clues. Recent research into some Neo-Assyrian (1000–500 BC) administrative records has revealed a high level of organisation within royal libraries, with acquisitions and accessions enthusiastically sought and carefully recorded. Literary works were arranged in terms of title and genre, the quantity in which the text was available and by description of its material. This could be in one of four categories: a full-sized clay tablet, divided into two or more columns; a smaller tablet, of just one column; a wax-covered writing board, consisting of two or more leaves; or a single-leaf writing board.

These records also make it clear that private collections in Babylonia were extensively used to build up the Ninevite private libraries, particularly after the fall of Babylon in 648 BC. Ashurbanipal himself supervised some of the acquisition, and a royal letter to the governor of Borsippa, explicitly commandeering all kinds of literary works from the temple and private libraries there, is almost certainly from him.

A wax-covered writing board in three parts, here shown opened out, found in a well at Nimrud. Each section was hinged so that it could be folded up.

The head of King Ashurbanipal, a detail of a limestone panel depicting a scene of warfare. It was in his library at Nineveh that most of the texts we have were discovered.

Because they were carefully excavated, the administrative archives of Ebla give a good insight into the nature and organisation of such archives. At Ebla tablets were stored on wooden shelves and were indexed. The contents or titles of individual tablets were recorded on the tablet edge to make them easier to find when stored on a shelf. If no shelves existed, tablets were placed in jars or baskets with an explanatory tag attached.

Literary tablets tended to have space reserved in the last column for a colophon. This contained the sort of information which a modern book provides on its title and imprint pages. The colophon might contain some of the following information: the title of the work; the name of the owner; the name of the scribe; the date of the work; comments on the original from which the scribe had copied; a declaration of secrecy; and an invocation of curses against any unauthorised person removing the tablet.

Sometimes the colophon was merely a shortened first line of the work in question plus the number of tablets in a series. For example, for the Epic of Gilgamesh it reads: 'Of him who found out all things [its first line] Tablet I, II, III [and so on].'

Texts were written in wedge-shaped cuneiform script on clay tablets, usually square or rectangular in shape, or sometimes on wooden boards. Clay was always readily available in Mesopotamia and easy to model into the required shape. The scribe used a stylus cut from a reed or perhaps one made of ivory or metal. It was trimmed at an angle or into a round end, either of which affected the style of the script. The scribe used the flat front side of the tablet first and, if necessary, continued on the back, which was slightly convex. After the tablet had been inscribed it was quite often just left to dry out, especially when the inscription was not intended for permanent record. Sometimes, however, it was baked so that it became virtually indestructible. Many of the tablets left unbaked in antiquity survive today, some of them only by lucky accident: the rooms where they were stored were deliberately burned by foreign conquerors and the heat thus baked the tablets, which might otherwise have gradually disintegrated in the damp conditions often prevalent in Iraq.

Only a very small percentage of the written material uncovered need concern us here, since most of it does not fall into the category of myth. Indeed, only a very small part of the whole corpus is 'literature' as we would understand it. Within this definition, however, we should include the few royal inscriptions, called 'Letters to the God' because of their introductory dedication and greeting to the god. Hard fact and pure historical information are perhaps their least merit, their content being selective, but they are distinguished by their highly poetic language. Particularly in descriptions of the prevailing countryside and the battles themselves, hyperbole paints a vivid picture. In his Letter to Ashur and the other gods who inhabit the city of Ashur, Sargon II describes his eighth campaign in 714 BC against Urartu, telling how his troops (with the help of the gods Shamash and Marduk) jumped the Lower Zab 'as if it were a ditch'. Simirra, 'a great finger of a mountain', is 'struck upright like the blade of a lance'. Battle troops are 'valiant eagles'. It is impossible to draw precise parallels, but this and other Letters to the God undoubtedly reflect established literary tradition. The Letters were probably intended to be read aloud to an audience; thus they are intense and alive, the action runs along apace, and their description of people, places and events is very realistic.

We should also consider a particular literary tradition which survived from Sumerian times: the Dialogue Text. This was a form of popular entertainment, which may even have been enacted or recited at court, whereby two opposing points of view were put forward by two personified contestants who argued their respective merits, e.g. The Tamarisk and the Palm, The Grain and the Wheat, The Ox and the Horse, Summer and Winter. These texts followed a stereotyped form; after an introduction saying who the disputants were and how they fitted into the great cosmological order, the grounds of their particular argument were established. Then came the contest proper, during which each side extolled its own merits while pointing out the failings of its adversary. The argument was referred to a god who pronounced judgement, which the two contestants readily accepted, departing from the scene the best of friends.

Relief showing King Sargon II in conference with a palace official.

This sort of competitive sparring was sometimes reflected in myth, as for example in Tablet VII of the Epic of Gilgamesh, when Enkidu first curses Shamhat the harlot with great curses ('The drunkard shall soak your party dress with vomit') and afterwards, following an intervention from the god Shamash, takes the polar opposite position:

'My utterance, which cursed you, shall bless you instead.
Governors and princes shall love you . . .'

Another form of dialogue potentially more intellectually satisfying, was a text we call the Babylonian Theodicy, although copies are extant from both Babylonia and Assyria. This is a dialogue in twenty-seven stanzas between a sceptic and a pious man, who alternately present their views on life in a polite and ceremonious way. Unfortunately, the dialogue is extremely repetitious and does not make much sense, ending somewhat lamely when the sceptic asks:

'May the god who has abandoned me give help
May the goddess who has forsaken me show mercy.'

The Dialogue of Pessimism presents perhaps the first instance of that situation comedy stand-by, the servant who is more nimble-witted than his master. To each of the twelve commands which the master issues, the servant replies with a witty riposte. When the command is countermanded, the servant neatly changes his riposte, showing there are two ways of looking at every situation. Some of the stanzas are somewhat abstruse, but it is clear that the intention was to amuse.

'Servant, obey me!'
'Yes, my lord, yes.'
'A woman will I love.'
'Yes, love, my lord, love. The man who loves a woman forgets pain and trouble.'
'No, servant, a woman I shall not love.'
'Do not love, my lord, do not love. Woman is a pitfall, woman is an iron dagger
 – a sharp one! – which cuts a man's neck.'

Such verbal wrestling occurs in conversations in myth, for example in Tablet VI of the Epic of Gilgamesh when the goddess Ishtar, overcome by Gilgamesh's beauty, offers herself to him along with a variety of rich rewards, only to be rejected in very colourful and exaggerated terms.

The Poor Man of Nippur is perhaps the most appealing tale outside the category of myth, with farcical overtones. The text was found at Sultantepe and a further fragment was uncovered from Ashurbanipal's library. It concerns a poor man taking revenge on the mayor of Nippur, who has taken his last goat. Three tricks are played, all of which result in the mayor receiving a sound beating, no doubt to the gratification of the audience. There is little repetition here and the fast-moving story points to the moral that those in high places have a duty to behave honestly.

The most important legacy of the literary tradition of ancient Mesopotamia, however, is its myths and legends, for which it was famed even in antiquity. We should perhaps define our terms here. If myths concern divine or semi-divine beings, legends concern historical or semi-historical beings. There are sufficient fragments extant to tell us there was a later epic tradition which related to the royal exploits of known historical kings, which we should describe as legends. But what concerns us here is myth: although Gilgamesh and Etana were known kings whose names appear on the Sumerian king list, they are, like Atrahasis and Adapa, semi-divine. Others of the myths recounted here solely concern the gods, in heaven and in the underworld, and great cosmological upheavals. The events described go back to the dawn of civilisation before – at least according to the Epic of Creation – there were any gods at all, nor any destinies decreed.

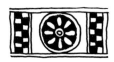

Gods and mortals, authors and audience

From around 3000 BC there is archaeological evidence for the beginning of walled cities in Mesopotamia, and for the building of temple complexes within them. These temples were built for the cult of a particular god; for example, the Sumerian city of Eridu for the god Enki. Because life was precarious, it was prudent for cities to be guarded by a special god who was responsible for both the city and its people. The temple was his house, and rituals of feeding, clothing and washing the god were carried out within the sanctuary. With the god lived his spouse and sometimes his children.

As more cities were built, the number of cult centres increased. Later cities adopted gods, made claims on their behalf and bestowed epithets on them with little regard for what had gone before. Some names and epithets were accretions of several early gods and goddesses. This meant the pantheon of gods, the basic structure of which went back to the third millennium, was full of paradox and repetition.

Gods

The more important and famous gods make frequent appearances in the myths. They include the following:

Anu, the sky-god, was originally chief god in Sumerian times. He was sometimes described as Ishtar's father. His spouse was **Antum** and his cult city was Uruk. **Ishtar** (Sumerian **Inanna**), the goddess of love, sex appeal and war, is described in one Sumerian text as the one whom not even 120 lovers could exhaust. Under various names she became the most important goddess throughout western Asia. Her sacred beast was the lion and her cult centres were at Uruk, Kish, Agade, and Arba'il.

Ellil, Anu's son, later replaced his father and became king of the gods. To him belonged the Tablet of Destinies by which the fates of men and gods were decreed. His spouse was **Mulliltu** or **Mylitta** (Ninlil) and his cult city was Nippur.

Ea (Sumerian **Enki**) was lord of the Apsu, the domain of sweet water beneath the earth. He was the source of all secret magical knowledge and instructed mankind in the arts and crafts. His spouse was **Damkina** and his cult centre was Eridu.

Imaginative reconstruction of Babylon in the time of Nebuchadrezzar II (605–562 BC), showing a bridge supported by five stone piers over the Euphrates, the great ziggurat on the left and to the right the temple of Marduk, Esagila.

Marduk was Ea's son. During the Kassite period he was elevated to the top of the Babylonian pantheon. His cult centre was naturally Babylon. **Nabu** was Marduk's son, the patron of scribes and a god of wisdom. His popularity reached a high point during the first millennium. His cult city was Borsippa.

Sin, the moon-god, was also described as Ishtar's father. He governed the passing of the months. His symbol was the crescent moon and he was worshipped at Ur and Harran. **Shamash** (Sumerian **Utu**), the sun-god, was judge of both heaven and earth. His symbol was the sun disk and his cult centres were Sippar and Larsa.

Adad, the weather-god, not only controlled storms but also the life-giving rain. His symbol was forked lightning and his animal the bull, which bellowed like thunder. **Dumuzi** (later known as **Tammuz**) was Ishtar's lover, a pastoral god. He protected seasonal fertility.

Impression (left) from a greenstone seal, showing the god Ea with water and fish streaming from his shoulders, his two-faced vizier to his left, to his right a bird (perhaps Anzu) and a winged Ishtar above the sun-god Shamash.

Cylinder seal impression (above) showing the sun-god Shamash with rays rising from his shoulders, and brandishing a saw, symbolic of his role as judge.

Impression from a chalcedony seal, showing a worshipper before the god Adad standing on his sacred bull. Winged human-headed bulls flank the shrine.

27

Black stone cylinder seal impression (right) showing the god Nergal, and dedicated to him. He brandishes his characteristic double lion-headed mace.

Impression (below) from a blue chalcedony seal showing a shaven-headed priest before the symbols of various deities.

Ereshkigal was the queen of the underworld. **Namtar** was her vizier, a much-feared god of plague who could let loose any one of sixty diseases. **Erra** or **Nergal** was the god of plague and war. **Ninurta** was a war-god and a patron of the hunt. He is the hero of the Epic of Anzu. **Nin-hursag** (also known as **Aruru** and **Mammi**) was the great mother goddess, sometimes described as the spouse of Nergal.

The **Annunaki** (**Anukki**) were the old Sumerian gods of fertility and the underworld, where they later became judges. The **Igigi**, often paired with the Annunaki, were the Sumerian group of sky-gods, headed by Ellil.

The temples in which the gods were worshipped were run by a priestly hierarchy, although we know very little about its precise arrangement. A priest called a *šatammu* probably headed the administrative side and another, an *en*-priest, the spiritual side. We know that sons often followed their fathers into priestly service one generation after another.

Throughout Mesopotamian history exorcists and diviners have played a significant part, and all over the ancient world the skills of the Babylonian diviners were very highly regarded. Techniques varied, but the more common ones were the observation of animals' entrails; the effect of oil on water; the pattern of smoke from incense; the behaviour of birds and other animals, especially about the city gates or within the temple precinct; and celestial and meteorological phenomena.

Religion played a great part in the everyday lives of ordinary people. On a personal level, they attached themselves to a particular god or goddess and offered prayers and sacrifices in return for intercession with the other gods and protection from evil spirits. There is a vast fund of spells and incantations, which sometimes used passages from myths. Even though ordinary people were denied access to the innermost sanctuaries of the temples, they were observers of the great religious processions. The enormous enclosure around the ziggurat at Babylon was probably designed to enable a large crowd to watch the ceremonies from a suitable distance.

Mesopotamian attitudes towards death are largely known from myths and epics. There was no promise of an afterlife, as in ancient Egypt, and it seems that death was accepted in a resigned and matter-of-fact way – the obvious exception being, as we shall see, Gilgamesh, who railed furiously against his friend's death which had been presaged by alarming dreams. The living made commemorative figurines of the dead, as Gilgamesh did for Enkidu. Burials, apart from early royal burials, took place in the house of the dead person, who was put under the floor with his favourite possessions. Corpses left unburied and denied the normal offerings of water by surviving relatives were thought to become restless ghosts who could harm the living. There were no public cemeteries.

Mortals

The people of Mesopotamia, even from earliest times, tended to live in cities. Apart from the basic advantage of security provided by numbers, this allowed the centralised organisation and maintenance of a canal network with artificial irrigation and drainage in a land where rainfall was extremely sparse. Despite the dry climate, the land was potentially very fertile and, regularly watered, could support several harvests a year. The principal crops were cereals and dates. The livestock included sheep, goats and cattle, and the soil was rich in clay which, when dried, was used not only for clay tablets but also for all building construction.

Early cities showed a pattern which repeated itself throughout Mesopotamian history. They consisted of three main parts: a walled inner area containing the temple, the palace, the houses of royal officials and those of citizens; the suburbs encompassing farms, fields, orchards and date groves; and the harbour area, which was the centre of commercial activity. Every city also

Ivory inlay from Megiddo
showing a victorious homecoming
and feasting.

had gates through the outer wall, and the area in front of these was used as a gathering place as well as for the transaction of business, law-giving and money-changing. This was also where scribes sold their skills.

The fortunes of cities periodically rose and fell, sometimes as a result of changes in water-courses. Even the splendour of a city such as Ur was intermittent: by the Middle Babylonian period, it was more or less a ruin. Larsa and Ashur disintegrated, though the latter revived in Parthian times, and the great city of Akkad literally disappeared without trace. Most cities only became truly rich and famous in periods of victory, when lavish spending was made possible by the spoils of war and luxury items such as spices, scent, wine, fine cloth and exotic animals reached them.

The inhabitants of cities could be divided into two main groups: those few who benefited from court and temple connections which gave them the use of their own means of production, and those who were wholly dependent on the temple and palace organisations. Most of the means of production were under the control of the vast temple complexes and the royal palaces, although private individuals owned land as well. Both temple and palace derived their income mainly from agriculture, either directly or through the payment of rates and taxes. Central administration received most income and redistributed it. Both organisations supported a large number of personnel who were 'paid' with food, clothing and so on.

Those who were dependent, to a greater or lesser extent, upon the temple and palace organisations can perhaps be categorised as peasants, craftsmen, slaves and merchants, whose exact status varied at different periods. A further

Cylinder seal impression
showing a ploughing
scene. Barley was the
principal crop.

Detail (above) from the palace reliefs of Ashurnasirpal at Nimrud, showing soldiers crossing a river by means of inflated animal skins.

Cylinder seal impression (left) showing a palace or temple facade with animals to the right.

very important class within this society was the scribes, whose calling always carried prestige. There is no definite evidence to tell us how candidates for this group were selected, but they were frequently the sons and relatives of city princes and governors. There is only one known instance of female scribes, at Mari, where evidence from lists of rations allotted to palace workers reveals some nine female names. Unfortunately there are no details of their social standing, training, or the type of work they did.

Peasants were engaged in a number of occupations, mainly agricultural. They sowed, reaped and threshed barley, sometimes several times a year where the land could support it. They also tended herds, mainly sheep and goats of several varieties. They milked cows, ewes and goats, and made butter and cheese. Farmyards usually contained ducks and geese; hens were common only in later periods. There was in addition a great deal of seasonal nomadism.

Craftsmen followed more varied occupations, many of which were hereditary, the skills being passed by father to son. Some were engaged in the cloth trade: bleaching, spinning and dyeing. There is archaeological evidence for spindle-whorls at all early settlements. Other craftsmen were tanners. Leather and skins were used in making shields and harnesses, small boats, drinking bags, pouches for milk and butter, and sandals. Skins were also inflated for crossing rivers.

Craftsmen could also be potters, although this occupation had a rather

Detail from bands of embossed bronze from the Balawat Gates in the reign of Shalmaneser III. Bound captives are brought to the capital.

low profile. As early as the sixth millennium, a large variety of rather dull pottery was being made throughout Mesopotamia. Potters' wheels were in widespread use soon after 4000 BC. More important were metal-workers. Before 7000 BC there is evidence that native copper was being made into simple tools, and by 6000 BC lead and copper were being smelted. There is evidence for metal casting during the latter part of the fifth millennium.

Carpenters made chariots, sledges and ploughs, and there were also stone-carvers, brewers, jewellers, scent-makers, confectioners, bakers and basket-makers.

As for slaves, these could be roughly divided into two categories: slaves belonging to private individuals and those owned by the temples or palaces. Those in the first group were often born or perhaps adopted into the house where they were enslaved. The famous Law Code of Hammurabi (king of Babylon from 1792 to 1750 BC) makes it apparent that, certainly in the Old Babylonian period, slaves enjoyed a special status. The Code also tells us that sometimes people sold themselves, their wives and children into slavery if they were unable to pay a debt. Once the debt was repaid, they regained their former status. While in slavery, their position was protected to some extent by the Code and their relationship with their masters was based on mutual obligation.

Many slaves came into the country as prisoners of war. Assyrian reliefs depict such people being led to the capital, often with their wives and children. Foreign slaves were particularly prized for their artistic skills, and often for the beauty of their women, but mainly their work was domestic, and they helped in the fields at harvest time.

The Old Testament speaks with loathing of the merchants of Babylon and Nineveh. These merchants occupied an important place in society, since Mesopotamia was poorly provided with mineral resources. As it lacked any stone suitable for building or for sculpture and had no gold, silver, copper or timber, or other precious items such as lapis lazuli, cornelian, rock crystal and turquoise, all these had to be acquired through trade. Trade was therefore crucial and the great rivers between which Mesopotamia lay, the Tigris and the Euphrates, served as major trading routes. Merchants engaged in two different types of trade: city and inter-city, and foreign trade, whereby textiles and food staples such as dates were traded for those commodities lacking in Mesopotamia, particularly metals.

Texts from Mari reveal routes which link the Mediterranean and Anatolia to the Persian Gulf. At that period trading caravans had royal protection and foreign merchants travelling from court to court were treated with honour. This, however, did not become the general situation in Mesopotamia until the time of Sargon II (721–705 BC). Not only did trade enhance living standards, it also served to spread the influence of Mesopotamian civilisation. With the exchange of goods doubtless went an exchange of ideas and stories.

Scribes were trained in schools which were nearly always attached to temples. There is a record of only one independent establishment, at Ur. Scribal training was long and repetitive and because of the very complexity

Mural painting of scribes, from Til Barsip on the Middle Euphrates in the reign of Tiglath-Pileser III (744–727 BC).

A typical school tablet, showing three registers of signs.

of cuneiform – over five hundred variable signs – it required not only application and patience, but intelligence. Teaching relied on the memorisation of lists of words and signs copied over and over again, and such training began early in boyhood. Even outside the borders of Mesopotamia scribes were carefully trained, and bi-lingual syllabaries and lexical lists have been found in the Hittite capital of Boğazköy.

The school curriculum was apparently standard and changed little over the millennia. A Sumerian literary document describes the reaction of a schoolboy and also the behaviour and attitude of his teachers and parents. Written perhaps as early as 2000 BC, it was a highly popular composition and repeatedly copied. The schoolboy in question read his tablet, ate his lunch, prepared and wrote another tablet, and was assigned oral and written work, but, unfortunately for him, his work was not up to standard and he was caned by various teachers. The boy's parents then invited his teacher home, where he was feasted and presented with gifts. After this his attitude changed; he waxed lyrical about his pupil's abilities and Nissaba, the goddess of schools and scribes, was exhorted to show favour to the boy's reed.

Authors

The scribes copied the texts, but who were the original authors of the creative literature? Unfortunately, any answers to this question are bound to be conjecture, since our evidence is meagre and has to be carefully interpreted.

The very fact that creative writing exists at all presupposes that there were individual authors at work, but cuneiform literature hardly ever names them. Traditionally, authorship of the oldest works was attributed to sages sent out before the Flood by the god Ea to bring civilisation to mankind. After the Flood, authors were honoured with sage-like status, which gave their work the strong foundations of great antiquity and divine inspiration. But these authors did not mention their own names and throughout the whole of Mesopotamian literature there are only two possible exceptions to this rule. The first is Kabti-ilani-Marduk, who professes to have drawn up the tablets of the Epic of Erra – although he says he received the entire work in a vision, which rather weakens his claim to original authorship. The author of the Epic of Gilgamesh is recorded in a first-millennium catalogue of cuneiform literature as Sin-leqi-unnini ('Oh-Sin-accept-my-prayer'), an exorcist-priest who probably lived in Uruk. His name has been traced back to the Middle Babylonian period (1600–1000 BC) when Babylon was ruled by the Kassites and, since this was a time when the epic was standardised, it is probable that Sin-leqi-unnini was the recorder of a definitive version rather than its original author. His version was influential enough, however, to ensure that his name is permanently associated with the epic.

It is perhaps not surprising that a civilisation which produced from earliest times syllabaries and lists of cuneiform signs, and bi-lingual tablets of Sumerian words with their Akkadian equivalents, should also have produced a catalogue of authors. Such a catalogue, albeit fragmentary and somewhat obscure, was found in Ashurbanipal's library. It lists works and ascribes them to named scholars, and also identifies four classes of authors: gods; legendary humans and humans of great antiquity; humans with no indication of family origin; and humans with indication of family origin, described as 'son' of an ancestral figure.

The first two categories underline that, in Mesopotamian eyes, true authenticity must derive from divine inspiration and/or great antiquity. These apart, there remain various names, all of whom are said to be scholars of particular cities and to possess priestly titles. It would be fascinating to trace both the ancestors and descendants of those names, with indications of family origin, but this would require a great deal more information than we have. The catalogue does, however, show that the Mesopotamians themselves were interested in the identity of the chief scribes of the temple schools and considered them to be the authors of the compositions.

In fact, even if the works in question were signed, it is probable that we would consider most of the versions we have as compilations rather than originals. It is clear that generations of story-tellers and scribes have added and omitted passages as seemed appropriate or topical at the time. Few works bear the imprint of a single personality. The Epic of Gilgamesh itself has been described as a 'stitch-up job', and it certainly reveals some techniques used to give cohesion and continuity to the whole. Sometimes the joins are less than smooth.

Audience

If the authors themselves are hard to trace, the identity of the audience or readers must be pure conjecture. We know that only a tiny percentage of the population were literate, and thus access to literature by the rest must have depended upon someone who could read, i.e. a scribe. So how did the general public indulge its taste for literature?

In the case of the Letters to the God described in the previous chapter, their style and content suggest that some at least were meant to be read out aloud to an assembly of citizens, rather than silently deposited in the sanctuary before an elite congregation. Some of the Letters show a careful build-up of tension: after the assessment of a deadly foe, a crisis when all looks hopeless, a sudden divine intervention brings sure triumph. Then there is the language which, as we have seen, is extremely stirring and full of vivid similes. There are also fanciful descriptions of the marvels of 'abroad'. This all points to an audience sophisticated enough to be aware not only of its own traditions but of the existence of others, and thus to be able to make comparisons and contrasts. Because of their trading links, Mesopotamians knew about foreign lands and were able to take a wide view of what was happening outside their own borders. As for the lively descriptions of the beauties of nature, this only makes sense if an audience is actively participating, and it is not hard to imagine gasps of wonder and amazement at some of the wilder flights of fanciful report. Sometimes there are quite technical details, of weaponry manufacture for example, and once more this points to an audience whose members included master craftsmen familiar, for example, with how much metal went into making a decent axe.

To refer to the audience as an 'assembly of citizens' is necessarily somewhat vague, since we cannot know exactly who was privileged enough to hear these readings. It probably depended to some extent on where they took place: at court, in temples at festivals, or even around caravan campfires. Clearly, different locations would have commanded different types of audiences.

But what of the audience for imaginative literature – the written versions of the myths and legends? Was it the same 'assembly of citizens' who heard the stories that we have uncovered from the ancient libraries, and which therefore bear the stamp of official acceptance? Or was this a more elite section of society – temple and palace personnel, for example?

These texts provided for us by the accident of discovery are subtle and esoteric, much more so than the Letters to the God. Although the locations in the stories can be specific (for example, Uruk and the Lebanon in the Epic of Gilgamesh, Babylon in the Epic of Creation and Nippur in the Epic of Anzu), and the plot can describe a definite historical event (for example, the building of Uruk's city walls and the foundation of Babylon), and the heroes can be famous and real people (for example, Gilgamesh and Etana), all are presented in an idealised fashion. There is little prosaic detail. Plots are unimportant; in some cases they are practically non-existent. The action moves slowly and is quite often halted altogether for consideration of the beauties of nature and the wonders of the cosmos, as well as the interpretation of highly cryptic dreams. All this results in a sophisticated form of literature not necessarily easy of access, especially when the added subtleties of language and style, the artful puns and elaborate repetition are taken into account.

This raises the question of a vernacular literature existing alongside the literary texts. Unfortunately, there is very little hard evidence for an oral tradition, but it must have existed. Isolated tablets surviving in single copies suggest an abundance of love songs, courtly tales and legends, topical, popular and bawdy stories, riddles, animal lore and parables. Probably versions of these were sung, told and performed not only at court but in more humble surroundings. The second-millennium royal courts at Ur, Isin, Larsa and Baby-lon harboured scholars and poets, and these places were probably centres of creativity in this genre at other times as well. And because of their ephemeral and topical nature, these stories may have been recorded (if at all) on something less durable than baked clay tablets. Papyrus and leather, for example, do not long survive damp conditions, and waxed boards are prone to damage.

It is possible that the preserved literary tradition may sometimes have been sung, to the accompaniment of a harp or lyre, by trained professionals who had learned the words by heart. As for public oratory, it is only the Epic of Creation which specifically states that it is to be recited – as part of the ritual on the fourth day of the New Year's Festival in Babylon.

That there is a connection between myth and ritual is certain, but fashions change in the interpretation of how close a link there is. Biblical scholars at the beginning of this century, influenced by the theories of J. G. Frazer, author of *The Golden Bough*, believed that all myths originated from rituals, but that view is now treated with more caution. We cannot know in many instances which came first, the myth or the ritual, and there are certainly myths in other cultures which have no apparent ritual association at all. The relationship between the two is complex and variable. In the Near Eastern context, it is important to bear in mind the possible ritual associations, but also to remember that except in specific cases – for example, in the last part of the Descent of Ishtar to the Underworld, where a fertility ritual involving the god Dumuzi is intended, and in the Epic of Creation – such connections may be slight, casual or even non-existent.

Gilgamesh and the Flood

Most of the twelve chapters of the Epic of Gilgamesh were found during the last century at Nineveh in the ruins of the temple of Nabu and at the palace library of Ashurbanipal. At the beginning of this century, Bruno Meissner purchased a large fragment of the epic from a dealer in Baghdad. It had been found in the ruins of ancient Sippar (modern Abu Habba) and contained part of the Old Babylonian version of Tablet x. Then, in 1914, the University of Pennsylvania bought from an antiquities dealer a fairly complete six-column tablet containing the Old Babylonian version of Tablet II. At about the same time, Yale University acquired from the same dealer a continuation of the Pennsylvania Tablet inscribed with Tablet III. Shortly before the First World War, a team of Germans excavating at Ashur found a considerable fragment of the Assyrian version of Tablet vi and, in the 1928–9 season, they discovered at Uruk two rather smaller pieces belonging to Tablet iv. Despite this serendipity, it is not possible to restore the entire epic without gaps, but we do have some three thousand lines of the main epic as well as four separate Sumerian stories, some parts of which are incorporated in Akkadian into the main epic.

We know almost certainly that Gilgamesh was a youthful ruler of Uruk during its First Dynasty (around 2600 BC). The Sumerian king-list assigns to him a reign of 126 years. He was said to be the son of the goddess Ninsun, whose husband was the king Lugalbanda. But although the epic says that Lugalbanda was Gilgamesh's father, the Sumerian king-list tells us his father was 'a high priest of Kullab' (a district within Uruk). This made Gilgamesh at least semi-divine. His most famous accomplishment was the building of the city walls around Uruk, mentioned in the epic and confirmed by a later ruler of the city, Anam, who recorded his own rebuilding of the walls which he described as 'an ancient work of Gilgamesh'.

The epic opens with a brief declaration of the deeds and fortunes of its hero, a scene-setting device which establishes Gilgamesh as great in knowledge and wisdom, as one who brought information from before the days of the Flood, and as one who went on a long journey in search of immortality, became weary and resigned, returned home and engraved on a tablet of stone all that he had done and suffered, and then completed the building of the walls of Uruk and its holy temple Eanna, the home of the goddess Ishtar.

This framework is then filled out with the story proper, which begins with a rampant Gilgamesh exercising *droit de seigneur* over all the nubile maidens in Uruk while forcing all its able-bodied young men to work on the city walls and the temple. Eventually the inhabitants of Uruk invoke the mother of the gods, Aruru, urging her to create a rival to Gilgamesh.

> Aruru washed her hands, pinched off a piece of clay, cast it out into open country.
> She created a primitive man, Enkidu the warrior: offspring of silence, sky-bolt
>   of Ninurta.
> His whole body was shaggy with hair, he was furnished with tresses like a woman,
> His locks of hair grew luxuriant like grain.
> He knew neither people nor country; he was dressed as cattle are.
> With gazelles he eats vegetation,
> With cattle he quenches his thirst at the watering place.
> With wild beasts he satisfies his need for water.

The primitive man Enkidu is one of the most important characters in the epic. But first he must be tamed. This is done by the harlot Shamhat; she reveals to him her many attractions and, after six days and seven nights of love-making, Enkidu is changed:

> Enkidu had been diminished, he could not run as before.
> Yet he had acquired judgement, had become wiser,
> He turned back, he sat at the harlot's feet.

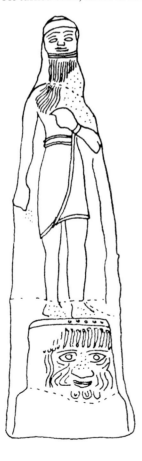

Possibly a representation of the hero Gilgamesh, standing on the head of the vanquished Humbaba. Despite the fact that this is the longest and best known myth, pictorial representations are scarce and difficult to verify.

The harlot was looking at his expression,
And he listened attentively to what the harlot said.
The harlot spoke to him, to Enkidu,
'You have become profound, Enkidu, you have become like a god.
Why should you roam open country with wild beasts?
Come, let me take you into Uruk the Sheepfold,
To the pure house, the dwelling of Anu and Ishtar,
Where Gilgamesh is perfect in strength,
And is like a wild bull, more powerful than any of the people.'

Enkidu agrees to go to Uruk so that he can challenge Gilgamesh and
show him that even one born in the open country can be superior in strength.
But Shamhat tries to persuade Enkidu that Gilgamesh wants to be his friend:

'Let me show you Gilgamesh, a man of joy and woe!
Look at him, observe his face,
He is beautiful in manhood, dignified,
His whole body is charged with seductive charm.
He is more powerful in strength of arms than you! He does not sleep by day
    or night.
O Enkidu, change your plan for punishing him!
Shamash loves Gilgamesh,
And Anu, Ellil, and Ea made him wise!
Before you came from the mountains,
Gilgamesh was dreaming about you in Uruk.'

Tablet I ends with two dreams of Gilgamesh, about a sky-bolt and a
star. Both are interpreted to mean that a strong partner will come to him
and that they will love one another. But despite these good auspices, Tablet
II begins with Enkidu in fighting form, waylaying Gilgamesh on his way to
yet another amorous assignment.

Enkidu blocked his access at the door of the father-in-law's house,
He would not allow Gilgamesh to enter.
They grappled at the door of the father-in-law's house,
Wrestled in the street, in the public square.
Door-frames shook, walls quaked.

The outcome of the wrestling match is that the two protagonists recognise
that they are not meant to fight but to be friends; almost immediately they
decide on a joint venture, to kill the giant of the Pine Forest, Humbaba (or
Huwawa in the earlier version), 'whose shout is the flood-weapon, whose
utterance is Fire, and whose breath is death'. The great counsellors of Uruk
advise against such a foolhardy plan of action, but at the beginning of Tablet
III they have become reconciled to the venture and their advice is practical.

'Do not trust entirely, Gilgamesh, in your own strength.
When you have looked long enough, trust to your first blow.
He who leads the way will save his comrade.
He who knows the paths, he will guard his friend.
Let Enkidu go in front of you,
He knows the way of the Pine Forest.
He can look at the fight and instruct in the battle.

The face of Humbaba, the giant of the Pine Forest.

Let Enkidu guard the friend, keep the comrade safe,
Bring him back safe in person for brides,
So that we in our assembly may rely on you as king,
And that you in turn as king may rely on us again.'

The exact location of the Pine Forest is not certain. An earlier Sumerian version of this part of the epic suggests that it was to the east of Mesopotamia, possibly near the Zagros mountains on the borders of Elam, but the later version states that it was to the west of Mesopotamia in the Lebanon. We do have some idea what Humbaba looked like: a clay head, probably from Sippar and now in the British Museum, bears an inscription saying it is he, and very unpleasant he is with his fat-encircled face.

Taking heed of the counsellors' words, Gilgamesh and Enkidu consult Ninsun, the great queen. She makes a smoke-offering to the sun-god Shamash for Enkidu to protect his friend so that Gilgamesh may return safely.

Tablet IV, unfortunately in bad condition, describes how the two friends set off, eat their rations, and set up camp. True to both epic tradition and his own character, Gilgamesh has two 'extremely upsetting' dreams, which Enkidu interprets to mean that their expedition against Humbaba will be successful.

Tablet V sees the arrival of the friends at Humbaba's lair. It is splendidly described for a Mesopotamian audience, to whom forests would not have been familiar:

They stood and admired the forest,
Gazed and gazed at the height of the pines,
Gazed and gazed at the entrance to the pines,
Where Humbaba made tracks as he went to and fro.
The paths were well trodden and the road was excellent.
They beheld the Pine Mountain, dwelling-place of gods, shrine of Irnini.
The pines held up their luxuriance even on the face of the mountain.
Their shade was good, filling one with happiness.
Undergrowth burgeoned, entangling the forest.

Humbaba approaches and is scornful of his visitors: 'You are so very small that I regard you as I do a turtle or a tortoise . . .'

All seems hopeless; Gilgamesh despairs. As we shall see, it is common in Mesopotamian myths that, just when disaster threatens, the gods intervene with divine weapons and turn the tables against the enemy.

Shamash summoned up great tempests against Humbaba,
South Wind, North Wind, East Wind, West Wind, Moaning Wind,
Gale, *saparziggu*-Wind, *imhulla*-Wind, . . .-Wind,
Asakku, Wintry Wind, Tempest, Whirlwind,
Thirteen Winds rose up at him and Humbaba's face grew dark.
He could not charge forwards, he could not run backwards.
Thus the weapons of Gilgamesh succeeded against Humbaba.

Humbaba pleads for his life, but Enkidu persuades Gilgamesh to finish him off. They decapitate the ogre and place his head on a raft which the Euphrates will carry down to Nippur.

Back in Uruk, Gilgamesh washes and changes into a clean robe and a sash. His glamour is too much for the goddess Ishtar:

And Ishtar the princess raised her eyes to the beauty of Gilgamesh.
'Come to me, Gilgamesh, and be my lover!
Bestow on me the gift of your fruit!
You can be my husband, and I can be your wife.
I shall have a chariot of lapis lazuli and gold harnessed for you,
With wheels of gold, and horns of *elmēšu*-stone

Cylinder seal (left) with its impression, showing a nude goddess, possibly a Syrian version of Ishtar, wearing elaborate jewellery.

You shall harness *ūmu*-demons as great mules!
Enter into our house through the fragrance of pine!
When you enter our house
The wonderfully-wrought threshold shall kiss your feet!'

But Gilgamesh is not tempted by the goddess and, with devastating frankness, lists the fates that have befallen her previous lovers: Dumuzi, still weeping; the colourful *allulu*-bird, whose wing she broke; the lion, for whom she dug seven-and-seven pits; the horse she whipped, goaded and lashed, and decreed that he should gallop seven leagues non-stop; the shepherd; the herdsman; the chief shepherd who was turned into a wolf; and lastly, her father's gardener, Ishullanu, who brought her baskets of dates, and whom she turned into a frog. 'And how about me? You will love me and then treat me just like them!'

Ishtar is not used to such plain speaking; she storms up to heaven and demands of her father, Anu, the Bull of Heaven to help her strike down Gilgamesh. Her terrible threats – 'I shall set my face towards the infernal regions, I shall raise up the dead, and they will eat the living, I shall make the dead outnumber the living!' – prevail, and she enters Uruk with the reins of the Bull of Heaven in her hand.

Down beside the river the Bull snorts, and a chasm opens up into which a hundred young men of Uruk fall, then two hundred, then three hundred. It snorts again and another chasm opens up, into which another hundred young men of Uruk fall, then two hundred, then three hundred.

> At its third snorting a chasm opened up,
> And Enkidu fell into it.
> But Enkidu leapt out. He seized the Bull of Heaven by the horns.
> The Bull of Heaven blew spittle into his face,
> With its thick tail it whipped up its dung.

Half-blinded, Enkidu calls on Gilgamesh, who plunges his sword into the Bull's neck. They pull out its innards.

> Ishtar went up on the wall of Uruk the Sheepfold.
> She was contorted with rage, she hurled down curses.
> 'That man Gilgamesh who reviled me has killed the Bull of Heaven!'
> Enkidu listened to Ishtar saying this,
> And he pulled out the Bull of Heaven's shoulder and slapped it into her face:
> 'If I could only get at you as that does,
> I would do the same to you myself,
> I would hang its intestines on your arms!'
> Ishtar gathered the crimped courtesans,
> Prostitutes and harlots.
> She arranged for weeping over the Bull of Heaven's shoulder.

Gilgamesh summons the craftsmen of Uruk to admire the horns and then to decorate them. He dedicates them to his father Lugalbanda. The two heroes wash in the Euphrates and ride in triumph through the streets of Uruk. This is the high point of the epic.

Impression from a blue chalcedony seal, possibly showing Gilgamesh and Enkidu slaying the Bull of Heaven, with the goddess Ishtar trying to prevent them.

Tablet VII is not well preserved and about twenty lines at the beginning are missing. Fortunately they can be partly filled in from a Hittite version, and they reveal Enkidu recounting his dream the morning after the great fight with the Bull of Heaven. The dream's portent is clear.

'O my brother, what a dream I saw last night!
Anu, Ellil, Ea, and heavenly Shamash were in the assembly.
And Ea said to Ellil, "As they have slain the Bull of Heaven,
So too they have slain Huwawa, who guarded the mountains planted with pines."
And Anu said, "One of them must die."
Ellil replied: "Let Enkidu die, but let Gilgamesh not die."'

Gilgamesh listens to his friend's words, 'and his tears flowed'. He goes to offer prayers to the great gods. Enkidu curses his fate, and particularly he curses Shamhat for corrupting him in the first place. Shamash replies on her behalf:

'Enkidu, why are you cursing my harlot Shamhat,
Who fed you on food fit for gods,
Gave you ale to drink, fit for kings,
Clothed you with a great robe,
Then provided you with Gilgamesh for a fine partner?
And now Gilgamesh, the friend who is a brother to you
Will lay you to rest on a great bed
And lay you to rest on a bed of loving care,
And let you stay in a restful dwelling, the dwelling on the left.
Princes of the earth will kiss your feet.
He will make the people of Uruk weep for you, mourn for you,

And he himself will neglect his appearance after your death.
Clothed only in a lionskin, he will roam the open country.'

Enkidu's anger abates; he forgives Shamhat. He falls ill and dreams
again of his own death and descent to the underworld. For twelve days he
lies in bed and grows weaker. In a moving speech at the beginning of Tablet
VIII, Gilgamesh bids farewell to his friend. He lists all who will weep for
him: the elders of Uruk, the open country, the field, the myrtle, pine and
cypress trees:

'They shall weep for you, the bear, hyena, leopard, tiger, stag, cheetah,
Lion, wild bulls, deer, mountain goat, cattle, and other wild beasts of the open
    country,
It shall weep for you, the pure Euphrates,
With whose water in waterskins we used to refresh ourselves.
They shall weep for you, the young men of the broad city, of Uruk the Sheepfold,
Who watched the fighting when we struck down the Bull of Heaven...'

But Enkidu can no longer hear:

'Now, what is the sleep that has taken hold of you?
Turn to me, you! You aren't listening to me!
But he cannot lift his head.
I touch his heart, but it does not beat at all.'

Enkidu has died and Gilgamesh sends a shout throughout the land, a
shout for a precious likeness to be fashioned of his friend, of copper, silver,
jewels, lapis lazuli and gold. The rest of the tablet is very broken but what
remains suggests that it is concerned with the funeral rites of Enkidu.

Tablet IX reveals a distraught Gilgamesh roaming the open country,
terrified of death. He decides to go to see Ut-napishtim, who with his wife
is supposed to have survived the Flood and to know the secret of eternal
life. The journey is hazardous: lions lurk in the passes, and the gate to the
towering mountain of Mashu, through which he must pass, is guarded by
Scorpion-men 'whose aura is frightful, and whose glance is death. Their terrifying mantles of radiance drape the mountains.'

At first Gilgamesh's reception is hostile, but in a very broken passage
he obviously manages to convince the Scorpion-man and his woman that
he must pass through their gate, even though:

'It is impossible, Gilgamesh...
Nobody has passed through the mountain's inaccessible tract.
For even after twelve leagues...
The darkness is too dense, there is no light.'

In a highly stylised passage in which three nearly identical lines are
repeated, building tension in a most effective way, Gilgamesh progresses
through this ancient slough of despond:

When he had achieved one [two/three/four etc.] leagues[s]
The darkness was dense, there was no light,
It was impossible for him to see ahead or behind.

Sculpture of a scorpion-man, with coiled tail and splayed pincers, from Tell Halaf in Syria.

The unknown audience can almost be sensed counting its way through the dark miles. Suddenly Gilgamesh comes out into bright sunshine and a jewelled garden, the description of which is unfortunately missing about twenty-four lines. It begins:

> All kinds of thorny, prickly, spiky bushes were visible, blossoming with gemstones.
> Carnelian bore fruit
> Hanging in clusters, lovely to look at,
> Lapis lazuli bore foliage,
> Bore fruit, and was delightful to view.

Many different kinds of trees and semi-precious stones are mentioned and in the distance can be glimpsed the sea, probably the Mediterranean off the Phoenician coast. There lives Siduri, the divine ale-wife.

Tablet x begins with an introduction to Siduri. Her profession of beer-seller is well attested in the second millennium. There is nothing of the jolly barmaid about her, however; she is almost a prophetess here. At first, when she sees Gilgamesh, she locks herself behind her door because she thinks he may be an assassin. Certainly he looks very different from the splendid young man in clean robes and a sash who proved so irresistible to Ishtar.

> Clad only in a lionskin ...
> He had the flesh of gods upon his body,
> But grief was in his innermost being.
> His face was like that of a long-distance traveller.

Gilgamesh accosts Siduri and tells her that he (and presumably Enkidu – the tablet is very fragmentary here) are the ones who destroyed Humbaba in the Pine Forest. The ale-wife seems to know all about them, including the killing of the Bull of Heaven, but she does not believe this can be Gilgamesh. He replies:

> 'How could my cheeks not be wasted, nor my face dejected,
> Nor my heart wretched, nor my appearance worn out,
> Nor grief in my innermost being,
> Nor my face like that of a long-distance traveller
> Nor my face weathered by cold and heat . . . ,
> Nor roaming open country, clad only in a lionskin?
> My friend whom I love so much, who experienced every hardship with me –
> Enkidu, whom I love so much, who experienced every hardship with me –
> The fate of mortals conquered him! Six days [and] seven nights I wept over him. . . .'

Gilgamesh then asks the ale-wife the way to Ut-napishtim, saying:

> 'If it possible, I shall cross the sea;
> If it is impossible I shall roam open country again.'

The ale-wife tells Gilgamesh that there has never been a ferry of any kind, from time immemorial, and that only Shamash has ever crossed the sea:

> 'The crossing is difficult, the way of it very difficult.
> And in between are lethal waters which bar the way ahead.'

She suggests that he look for the boatman, Ur-shanabi, beside the lethal waters and persuade him to take him across.

Straightaway Gilgamesh goes in search of Ur-shanabi, and it seems as if there is some kind of affray, but the text is very fragmentary here, and when it resumes, Ur-shanabi has taken up Siduri's refrain:

> 'Why are your cheeks wasted, your face dejected,
> Your heart so wretched, your appearance worn out . . .'

Gilgamesh replies as he did to Siduri and concludes with the same request for directions to Ut-napishtim. In reply, Ur-shanabi tells Gilgamesh he must cut down three hundred poles, each 100 ft (30 m) long. These are to help them cross the lethal waters. They set off, using one pole at a time, Ur-shanabi warning Gilgamesh on no account to let the lethal water wet his hand. As they approach, Ut-napishtim sees them and begins to soliloquise, but unfortunately there is a break in the text of some twenty lines here. After the gap, Ut-napishtim asks Gilgamesh, in exactly the same words as those already used by Siduri and Ur-shanabi, why his cheeks are wasted and his face dejected. Gilgamesh replies exactly as he did to them, concluding with a passage on his long and difficult journey thus far. Ut-napishtim replies:

> 'Why do you prolong grief, Gilgamesh?
> Since the gods made you from the flesh of gods and mankind,
> Since the gods made you like your father and mother,
> Death is inevitable at some time . . .'

Ut-napishtim then makes what is probably the most profound speech of the epic in an attempt to explain death to Gilgamesh:

> 'Nobody sees Death,
> Nobody sees the face of Death,
> Nobody hears the voice of Death.
> Savage Death just cuts mankind down.
> Sometimes we build a house, sometimes we make a nest,
> But then brothers divide it upon inheritance,
> Sometimes there is hostility in the land,
> But then the river rises and brings flood-water.
> Dragonflies drift on the river,
> Their faces look upon the face of the Sun.
> But then suddenly there is nothing.
> The sleeping and the dead are just like each other,
> Death's picture cannot be drawn.'

Tablet XI (the so-called Flood Tablet) begins with Gilgamesh wondering how it is that he and Ut-napishtim look just the same, yet one is mortal and the other immortal. Ut-napishtim's response is to tell him about the Flood and, to anyone familiar with the story of Noah's Ark, the parallels are many.

The gods decide to impose a great flood on mankind. Only Ea breaks rank to warn Ut-napishtim of the approaching doom. He sends a message via a reed hut and a brick wall:

> 'Man of Shuruppak, son of Ubara-Tutu,
> Dismantle your house, build a boat.
> Leave possessions, search out living things.
> Reject chattels and save lives!
> Put aboard the seed of all living things, into the boat.'

The great boat is then constructed, according to very precise measurements, and launched. Ut-napishtim relates to Gilgamesh how:

> 'I loaded her with everything there was,
> Loaded her with all the silver,
> Loaded her with all the gold,
> Loaded her with all the seed of living things, all of them.
> I put on board the boat all my kith and kin.
> Put on board cattle from open country, wild beasts from open country, all kinds
>   of craftsmen.'

The terrible flood arrives, and:

> 'For six days and seven nights
> The wind blew, flood and tempest overwhelmed the land;
> When the seventh day arrived the tempest, flood and onslaught
> Which had struggled like a woman in labour, blew themselves out.
> The sea became calm, the *imhullu*-wind grew quiet, the flood held back.
> I looked at the weather; silence reigned,
> For all mankind had returned to clay.
> The flood-plain was flat as a roof.
> I opened a porthole and light fell on my cheeks.
> I bent down, then sat. I wept.'

Ut-napishtim puts out first a dove, then a swallow, and both come back. Finally he sends a raven, which does not return, thereby showing that the waters have receded. (In the Bible, Noah sent out a raven first, then two doves.) He then makes a huge sacrifice to the great gods and, after some quarrelling among themselves, Ellil makes Ut-napishtim and his wife immortal, saying:

> 'Until now Ut-napištim was mortal,
> But henceforth Ut-napištim and his woman shall be as we gods are...'

His story ended, Ut-napishtim turns his attention to Gilgamesh's immortality and suggests he begin by a trial — not sleeping for six days and seven nights — the length of time that the flood lasted. But Gilgamesh fails the test; as soon as he is sitting down, 'Sleep breathed over him like a fog'. When Gilgamesh awakes after seven nights, he refuses to believe he has been asleep until he sees seven loaves of bread, some in a distinctly mouldy state, that have been placed by his head at the end of each night's sleep.

Disheartened, Gilgamesh determines to abandon his quest for immortality. Ut-napishtim tells Ur-shanabi to bring Gilgamesh a wash-bowl so that he may wash his hair and body.

> 'Put a new headband on his head.
> Have him wear a robe as a proud garment
> Until he comes to his city,
> Until he reaches his journey's end,
> The garment shall not discolour, but stay absolutely new.'

Ur-shanabi and Gilgamesh set off back across the lethal waters, but Gilgamesh does not leave empty-handed. To the people of the eastern Mediterranean the parting gift to a stranger homeward bound bestowed honour on both giver and receiver. (In Homer's *Odyssey* Menelaus and Helen gave parting gifts to Telemachus, and, in the Egyptian myth The Shipwrecked Sailor, the hero is not allowed to leave the island on which he has been washed up until his departure has been made honourable by the bestowal of lavish presents.) Ut-napishtim's parting gift to Gilgamesh is a 'closely guarded matter', a 'secret of the gods' — a plant of rejuvenation. Gilgamesh finds the plant, as directed, at the bottom of the sea, retrieves it and sets off on his journey to Uruk. But after thirty leagues, while washing one evening in a cool pool, a snake smells the sweet-scented plant and carries it off. 'Then Gilgamesh sat down and wept.' He realises that immortality is not to be his: 'I shall give up.'

Gilgamesh, still accompanied by Ur-shanabi, arrives once again at Uruk, and Gilgamesh proudly points out his true achievement, the magnificent city walls: 'Three square miles and the open ground comprise Uruk.'

There the epic probably ended. The last Tablet seems to have been an after-thought; it does not fit harmoniously with the rest of the epic because in it Enkidu is still alive, when we know he died in Tablet VII. In this final Tablet Gilgamesh makes two wooden objects, a *pukku* and a *mekku* (exactly what these are we do not know), and they fall into the underworld. Enkidu descends into the underworld to retrieve them for Gilgamesh but fails to follow his instructions, and so cannot return to the land of the living (a popular motif). Gilgamesh goes from god to god trying to secure Enkidu's release, which eventually he achieves, whereupon Enkidu is able to tell his friend all about the gloomy conditions in the underworld. Thus the epic ends in a sombre mood, very different from that at the end of Tablet XI, where a reconciled Gilgamesh realises that his perpetual memory is ensured by his magnificent building work.

The myth of Atrahasis

The Flood story is also preserved in another Akkadian myth. Atrahasis, according to one version of the Sumerian king-list, was the son of Ubara-Tutu, king of Shuruppak (modern Tell Fara in middle Mesopotamia), who is mentioned in Tablet XI of the Epic of Gilgamesh as being the father of Ut-napishtim. In fact, Atrahasis ('Extra Wise') and Ut-napishtim ('He Found Life') are both precursors of the biblical 'Noah'; there is also a Sumerian equivalent, Ziusudra ('Long Life'). Atrahasis is thus a universal figure of great antiquity.

The myth begins with the gods (rather than men) having to do all the hard work, digging out canals and clearing channels, and they do not like it. After 3,600 years they decide they have had enough and arm themselves to confront Ellil. Ellil dislikes being threatened in the middle of the night

Sculpture of a recumbent human-headed bull. Massive winged bulls and lions decorated and guarded the entrances to palaces and temples.

and his face goes as yellow as tamarisk. He summons the great gods to hear their case, and they decide that Belet-ili, the womb-goddess, shall create mortals, who will then do all the heavy work instead. This she does, creating seven males and seven females. From this small beginning grew a large population, too large for Ellil:

> 600 years, less than 600, passed,
> And the country became too wide, the people too numerous.
> The country was as noisy as a bellowing bull.
> The God grew restless at their racket,
> Ellil had to listen to their noise.
> He addressed the great gods,
> 'The noise of mankind has become too much,
> I am losing sleep over their racket.'

Ellil tries plague, he tries drought, he tries famine. Atrahasis tries to ensure that they do not work. The Standard and Old Babylonian versions differ, but eventually the effect of each of these three is devastating: after six years, the people are eating their daughters, and they can no longer carry out the hard work for which they were created. Enki and Ellil quarrel over the best course of action. Ellil decides to perform a 'bad deed' (the Flood), and Enki warns Atrahasis, giving him specific instructions for the boat he is to build, and warning him that the Flood will last for seven days.

> The Flood roared like a bull,
> Like a wild ass screaming the winds howled
> The darkness was total, there was no sun.

Unfortunately, at the climax of the action (and just where it would be fascinating to make comparisons with both the Epic of Gilgamesh and the Bible) there is a large gap of about fifty-eight lines, and the story only resumes at a point (similar to the one in the Epic of Gilgamesh) where the gods are gathering over the sacrifice made by Atrahasis, quarrelling as to who is to blame. Enki takes the credit for disclosing to Atrahasis what was in store, but in the very fragmentary ending it seems to be agreed that some sort of curb on man's reproduction is needed. The responsibility for this is to fall upon women, whose fertility is to be restricted, sometimes through barrenness and sometimes deliberately in certain social categories (such as temple prostitutes).

The epic ends with a hymnic summary, probably spoken by Ellil:

> 'How we sent the Flood.
> But a man survived the catastrophe.
> You are the counsellor of the gods;
> On your orders I created conflict.
> Let the Igigi listen to this song
> In order to praise you,
> And let them record your greatness.
> I shall sing of the Flood to all people:
> Listen!'

The Epic of Creation

The Epic of Creation, unlike that of Gilgamesh, appears to have been almost unknown outside Mesopotamia. Tablets have been found at Sultantepe, Nineveh, Kish and Babylon, but (again unlike the Epic of Gilgamesh) they show little variation. It is an epic only in that it deals with cosmological events; there are no mortal heroes and, as we shall see, little drama and no cliff-hanging suspense. It is more in the nature of a sacred book and was recited during the celebrations of the New Year's Festival at Babylon.

The epic begins at the very beginning of time,

> When skies above were not yet named
> Nor earth below pronounced by name, ...

and there are just two gods: Apsu, who represents the primordial waters under the earth, and Tiamat, who is the personification of the sea. They beget four generations of gods who, as in the myth of Atrahasis, become extremely noisy and their noise becomes unbearable:

> The gods of that generation would meet together
> And disturb Tiamat, and their clamour reverberated.
> They stirred up Tiamat's belly,
> They were annoying her by playing inside Anduruna*.
> Apsu could not quell their noise ...
>
> *a name of the god's dwelling

Apsu confronts Tiamat, who is inclined to be indulgent towards her noisy offspring, and in a loud voice he declares:

> 'Their ways have become very grievous to me,
> By day I cannot rest, by night I cannot sleep.
> I shall abolish their ways and disperse them!
> Let peace prevail, so that we can sleep.'

Tiamat is enraged, but Apsu plots with his vizier, Mummu, to put an end to their troublesome ways. Before they can put their plot into effect, however, it is discovered by Ea 'who knows everything'. He intervenes, puts Apsu and Mummu into a deep sleep and then slays them. Ea assumes the belt, the crown and the mantle of radiance and, well satisfied, retires to his private quarters.

Ea takes over the dwelling-place of Apsu as his own domain, and there he and his spouse Damkina create Marduk, superlative in every way:

Two ugallu-demons in combat (above), and an impression (below) from a black-and-white speckled diorite seal, showing a god standing on a mušhuššu-dragon. An interceding god presents a worshipper who carries a sacrificial animal.

Cylinder seal impression (above) showing a bearded lahmu-hero, hair parted in the middle and curls arranged in three sets either side of the face. He takes part in a contest scene.

Cylinder seal impression (below) showing bull-men in a contest scene.

He suckled the teats of goddesses;
The nurse who reared him filled him with awesomeness.
Proud was his form, piercing his stare,
Mature his emergence, he was powerful from the start.
Anu his father's begetter beheld him,
And rejoiced, beamed; his heart was filled with joy.
He made him so perfect that his godhead was doubled.
Elevated far above them, he was superior in every way.
His limbs were ingeniously made beyond comprehension.
Impossible to understand, too difficult to perceive.
Four were his eyes, four were his ears;
When his lips moved, fire blazed forth.
The four ears were enormous
And likewise the eyes; they perceived everything.
Highest among the gods, his form was outstanding.

Tiamat is disturbed and heaves about restlessly. The gods plot evil in their hearts and persuade Tiamat that she should avenge the death of Apsu.

Tiamat creates a troop of fearsome monsters:

> She stationed a horned serpent, a *mušhuššu*-dragon, and a *lahmu*-hero,
> An *ugallu*-demon, a rabid dog, and a scorpion-man,
> Aggressive *ūmu*-demons, a fish-man, and a bull-man.

Foremost among her monsters is Qingu, on whom she confers leadership of the army. She sets him upon a throne, addresses him as 'her only lover' and gives him the Tablet of Destinies. This ultimate honour bestows on its owner supreme power.

Tablet II begins with Tiamat marshalling her battle force and news of this reaching Ea, who 'was dumbfounded and sat in silence'. To his father Anshar he describes Tiamat's giant snakes, which are:

> 'Sharp of tooth and unsparing of fang.
> She filled their bodies with venom instead of blood.
> She cloaked ferocious dragons with fearsome rays,
> And made them bear mantles of radiance . . .'

He then repeats word for word the list of monsters, and the giving of the Tablet of Destinies to Qingu. Anshar is certainly worried: he twists his fingers, bites his lip, his liver is inflamed and his belly will not rest. He roars at Ea, 'You must be the one who declares war!'

In the gap which follows, we can assume that Ea goes forth to do battle with Tiamat, and fails, because then Anshar addresses Anu in similar terms. In another fragmentary part, it is clear that Anu sets forth but he too fails.

> Anshar was speechless, and stared at the ground;
> He gnashed his teeth and shook his head [in despair] at Ea.
> Now the Igigi assembled, all the Anukki.
> They sat silently [for a while], tight-lipped.

Finally they spoke:

> Will no [other] god come forward? Is fate fixed?

This is Marduk's moment. From his secret dwelling, Ea calls out an answer:

> 'The mighty heir who was to be his father's champion,
> Who rushes [fearlessly] into battle: Marduk the Hero!'

Marduk rejoices; he approaches Anshar, whose heart is filled with joy. Setting aside his trepidation, he kisses Marduk on the lips. Marduk is confident:

> 'Father, my creator, rejoice and be glad!
> You shall soon set your foot upon the neck of Tiamat!'

But he lays down one condition: if he is successful in defeating Tiamat and saving their lives, he demands to take over as supreme god:

> 'My own utterance shall fix fate instead of you!
> Whatever I create shall never be altered!
> The decree of my lips shall never be revoked, never changed!'

Anshar convenes a meeting of the gods so that they can be told in repetitive detail about all of Tiamat's doings, of the threat she presents, and of the arrival of Marduk and of the condition he has made. The gods duly assemble at a banquet:

> They became very carefree, they were merry,
> And they decreed destiny for Marduk their champion.

Despite their confidence in him, they first give him a test:

> They set up in their midst one constellation,
> And then they addressed Marduk their son,
> 'May your decree, O lord, impress the gods!
> Command to destroy and to recreate, and let it be so!
> Speak and let the constellation vanish!
> Speak to it again and let the constellation reappear.'
> He spoke, and at his word the constellation vanished.
> He spoke to it again and the constellation was recreated.
> When the gods his fathers saw how effective his utterance was,
> They rejoiced, they proclaimed: 'Marduk is King!'

Marduk fashions his weapons for the great battle: a bow and arrow, a mace in his right hand, lightning before him, and an ever-blazing flame in his body. He also makes a net to encircle Tiamat and marshals seven winds to go behind him to create turmoil inside Tiamat. Then he raises his great flood-weapon and mounts 'the frightful, unfaceable storm-chariot'; its team of four are called 'Slayer', 'Pitiless', 'Racer' and 'Flyer', and their teeth carry poison.

Radiant with terror, Marduk sets out on the road to Tiamat, but at the sight of her his will crumbles and he cannot decide what to do. Although this seems somewhat unrealistic, it is a common mythical device (used also in the Epic of Gilgamesh) to heighten tension, by putting the inevitable victory temporarily in the balance. Tiamat sneers, and Marduk's courage returns. He challenges Tiamat to single combat. Here is the climax, the great battle scene towards which everything has been leading:

> Face to face they came, Tiamat and Marduk, sage of the gods.
> They engaged in combat, they closed for battle.
> The Lord spread his net and made it encircle her,
> To her face he dispatched the *imhullu* -wind, which had been behind:
> Tiamat opened her mouth to swallow it,
> And he forced in the *imhullu* -wind so that she could not close her lips.
> Fierce winds distended her belly;
> Her insides were constipated and she stretched her mouth wide.
> He shot an arrow which pierced her belly,
> Split her down the middle and split her heart,
> Vanquished her and extinguished her life.
> He threw down her corpse and stood on top of her.

The gods who had formed part of Tiamat's terrifying army then panic and turn tail, but they are caught by Marduk and bundled into the net, where they cower:

And as for the dozens of creatures, covered in fearsome rays,
The gang of demons who all marched on her right,
He fixed them with nose-ropes and tied their arms.

Qingu is dispatched and the Tablet of Destinies is wrested from him.
Marduk seals it with his own seal and presses it to his breast. Then he turns
his attention once more to Tiamat:

The Lord trampled the lower part of Tiamat,
With his unsparing mace smashed her skull,
Severed the arteries of her blood. . .

He then slices her in half 'like a fish for drying'; from half of her he makes
a roof for the sky, and from the other half he makes the earth which keeps
out the subterranean waters below. On it he builds the large temple of Esharra
where he founds cult centres for Anu, Ellil and Ea.

Next Marduk proceeds to organise the rest of the universe: naming the
months of the year, apportioning to them three stars each, fashioning stands
for the great gods, making the crescent moon appear and designating it 'the
jewel of night to mark out the days'. From Tiamat's spittle, he makes scudding
clouds, wind and rain. From her poison, he makes billowing fog. From her
eyes, he opens the Euphrates and the Tigris.

*Drawing taken from a cylinder seal
showing Marduk and a subdued
mushussu-dragon, one of the monsters
recruited by Tiamat. Here Marduk holds
the rod and ring of kingship in his left
hand. His robe is decorated with
medallions and he wears an elaborate
crown.*

The gods are overcome with gratitude and prepare a reception for Marduk, at which Anu, Ellil and Ea give him presents. They dress him in gorgeous robes and bestow kingship on him. In return, Marduk tells them:

'Over the Apsu, the sea-green dwelling,
In front of Esharra, which I created for you,
[Where] I strengthened the ground beneath it for a shrine,
I shall make a house to be a luxurious dwelling for myself
And shall found his [Marduk's] cult centre within it,
And I shall establish my private quarters, and confirm my kingship.
Whenever you come up from the Apsu for an assembly,
Your night's resting place shall be in it, receiving you all.
Whenever you come down from the sky for an assembly,
Your night's resting place shall be it it, receiving you all.
I hereby name it Babylon, home of the great gods.
We shall make it the centre of religion.'

But Marduk's work is not yet finished. He makes up his mind to perform miracles and tells Ea his plan:

'Let me put blood together, and make bones too.
Let me set up primeval man: Man shall be his name.'

As in the myth of Atrahasis, man is to be created to do the work of the gods so that the gods can be at leisure. Divine revenge is wreaked on Qingu's

Reconstruction of the ziggurat at Babylon, and its ground plan.

corpse and mankind is created from his blood. Then Marduk divides the gods into those of the sky and those of the underworld. In gratitude, the gods offer themselves to build the night's resting place, of which Marduk has already spoken. Marduk is enthusiastic:

> His face lit up greatly, like daylight.
> 'Create Babylon, whose construction you requested!
> Let its mud bricks be moulded, and build high the shrine!'

This is to be the last work the gods will have to perform. For an entire year they manufacture bricks, and by the end of the second year they have built the great shrine and ziggurat of Esagila. To celebrate, Marduk holds a banquet and he is proclaimed king of the gods. The epic then ends with the enumeration of fifty honorific names of Marduk, with esoteric explanations of each one.

Much of the Epic of Creation is concerned with religious matters, which accounts for its rather unexciting style. It is highly repetitive and its message arcane. There is no introductory invitation, as in the Epic of Gilgamesh, for the audience to share the story, and in literary terms it is more heraldic, less narrative, and has a rich vocabulary within the elevated hymnic style. Perhaps it should be viewed primarily as a work to be read and enacted within a religious setting, and less as one intended to entertain.

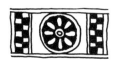

Shorter myths

The Epic of Creation, described in the previous chapter, told of the rise of Marduk to pre-eminence in the pantheon of gods. The Epic of Erra, probably composed during the ninth to eighth centuries BC, presents a very different picture of Marduk the Hero, here seen as senile, impotent and shambling. Scribes and poets had an awkward time explaining why Babylon, once so glorious, was now abandoned by its god and conquered by enemies, and perhaps for this reason the work is strikingly polemical and rhetorical.

In fact, the epic contains some dramatic descriptive passages about both the effects of war and pestilence, which are the work of Erra, and the blessings of peace and prosperity, which are assured for Babylon when its city-god is returned to his rightful place. Admittedly, the plot is almost non-existent, and the epic makes little attempt to describe events in sequence; instead the three protagonists – Erra, the good vizier Ishum, and Marduk – each take centre stage in turn, and declaim individually at length.

The Epic of Erra

The epic begins with the formula also encountered in the Epic of Anzu: 'I sing of the son of the king of all populated lands ...', a prologue addressed to Erra and Ishum. Erra, 'warrior of the gods, was stirring at home', his heart urging him to make war. Erra (also known as Nergal) is the god of plague and lord of the underworld. Such was his reputation that extracts of the epic later appeared on amulet-shaped clay tablets; these were hung on the walls of houses to ward off pestilence and protect the inhabitants.

Despite his warlike mood, Erra is assailed by lethargy and cannot make himself act. He tells his weapons to 'Stay propped in the cupboard!'. But these weapons – of whom the Sebitti, seven warrior gods who march at his side, are paramount – take him to task:

> 'Why do you stay in town like a feeble old man?
> How can you stay at home like a lisping child?
> Are we to eat women's bread, like one who has never marched on to the battlefield?
> Are we to be fearful and nervous as if we had no experience of war?
> To go on to the battlefield is as good as a festival for young men!'

They complain that they will soon be unfit for war:

Clay amulet inscribed with the Epic of Erra. Amulets had a magical function, and this particular one would have been hung in a house to protect the family from the plague (personified by Erra). The text is shown the right way up, although the suspension loop is at the bottom.

'And we, who know the mountain passes, we have quite forgotten the road!
Spiders' webs are spun over our campaign gear.
Our trusty bows have rebelled and become too tough for our strength.
The points of our sharp arrows are blunt.
Our daggers are corroded with verdigris for lack of butchery.'

Warrior Erra is inspired by their words, as pleasing to him 'as the best oil'. He tells his vizier Ishum to lead the way. Ishum demurs, but Erra's mind is made up, and he decides to confront Marduk. Entering Esagila, Marduk's temple in Babylon, he tells him without preamble that his finery is dirty and his crown tarnished. This is a ruse to get Marduk out of the way. Marduk explains that the craftsmen needed to restore his insignia to their former glory are now in the domain of sweet water beneath the earth and cannot come back up. Erra persuades Marduk to go down to them, promising that meanwhile he will rule and keep firm control of heaven and earth. Marduk duly sets off.

In Marduk's absence Erra plots to devastate Babylonia, making her cities a wilderness, desecrating her holy shrines, turning her royal palaces into ruins, and sowing conflict within families. Ishum intervenes and twice tries, ineffectually, to make Erra change his mind. On his third attempt, he passionately describes the unnatural effect of the destruction of Babylon:

'He who is ignorant of weapons is unsheathing his dagger,
He who is ignorant of battle is making war,
He who is ignorant of wings is flying like a bird. The weakling covers the master
    of force;
The fatty is overtaking the sprinter.'

Ishum reports that Marduk himself has cried 'Woe!' and clutched at his heart. All over Babylonia, in Sippar, Uruk, and Der, people are at war and the country violated. He concludes:

'O warrior Erra, you have put the just to death,
You have put the unjust to death.
You have put to death the man who sinned against you.
You have put to death the man who did not sin against you.
You have put to death the en-priest who made *taklimu*-offerings promptly,
You have put to death the courtier who served the king,
You have put old men to death on the porch,
You have put young girls to death in their bedrooms.
Yet you will not rest at all . . .'

Erra is defiant and he addresses all the gods:

'Keep quiet, all of you, and learn what I have to say!
What if I did intend the harm of the wrong I have just done?
When I am enraged, I devastate people!'

Ishum soothes him:

'Warrior, be still and listen to my words!
What if you were to rest now, and we would serve you?
We all know that nobody can stand up to you in your day of wrath!'

Appeased, Erra retires to his temple in Kutha. Ishum gathers the scattered people of Akkad, foretelling victory and prosperity for them as well as a time when they will look back and remember the devastation that once befell them.

'For countless years shall the praises of the great lord Nergal and the warrior Ishum
    [be sung]:
How Erra became angry and set his face towards overwhelming countries and
    destroying their people,
But Ishum his counsellor placated him so that he left a remnant!'

And Erra concludes:

'Let this song endure forever, let it last for eternity!
Let all countries listen to it and praise my valour!
Let settled people see and magnify my name!'

Etana

This myth concerns a very early king of Kish, whose name appears in the Sumerian king-list. A fable about an eagle and a snake who inhabit the same tree is incorporated with a central motif of a childless king who searches for a magical plant to ensure an heir. It is the only Mesopotamian myth

Impression from serpentine cylinder seal showing Etana sitting on the back of the eagle.

for which illustrations have been recognised: cylinder seals of the Akkadian period (2390–2249 BC) depict the episode in which Etana ascends towards heaven on the eagle's back. It is possible that the quarrel between the eagle and the snake was once an animal fable in its own right; the Sumerian story Gilgamesh and the Halub Tree, which tells of a snake and a bird which inhabit a poplar tree, may support this theory.

Tablet I begins with the foundation of the city of Kish, in which the great gods, both the Igigi and the Annunaki, have played a part. Ishtar is searching high and low for a king, and Ellil is looking for a throne-dais. Unfortunately, the last 120 lines are missing, but we can assume that, between them, Ellil and Ishtar ensure that Etana ascends the throne.

Tablet II introduces the eagle and the snake, who live in a poplar within the shade of the throne-dais. The two make a pact not to overstep the limit set by Shamash, and for some time live harmoniousiy, taking it in turns to catch prey which they share between themselves and their young. But once the eagle's young have grown large and flourished:

> The eagle plotted evil in its heart,
> And in its heart it plotted evil,
> And made up its mind to eat its friend's young ones.

Instantly the eagle receives a warning:

> A small fledgling, especially wise, addressed its words to the eagle, its father,
> 'Father, don't eat! The net of Shamash will ensnare you.
> The snares [on which] the oath of Shamash [is sworn] will overturn you and ensnare you.'

But the eagle will not be warned. It waits until evening, then goes down and eats the snake's young ones. The snake comes back, carrying its load of meat, and stares at its nest, 'Stared, for its nest was not there.'

The snake waits all night for the eagle, and in the morning weeps and appeals to Shamash:

> 'I trusted in you, Shamash the warrior,
> And I was helpful to the eagle who lives on the branches.
> Now the serpent's nest is grief-stricken.
> My own nest is not there, while its nest is safe.
> My young ones are scattered and its young ones are safe.
> It came down and ate my young ones!
> You know the wrong which it has done me, Shamash!
> Truly, O Shamash, your net is as wide as earth,
> Your snare is as broad as the sky!
> The eagle should not escape from your net . . .'

Shamash is not deaf to the appeal, and instructs the serpent to seek a wild bull (which is waiting, bound up), to open its insides and to hide itself within the bull's stomach. Birds of all kinds will come to eat the flesh and the eagle will be among them. When the eagle itself is feeding, the snake is to seize it by the wing, cut its wings, and throw the bird into a bottomless pit where it will be left to die of hunger and thirst.

All goes according to plan, although the exceptionally wise young fledgling again tries to deter its father ('Don't go down, father; perhaps the serpent is lying in wait inside this wild bull!'). Once again it is overruled and soon the eagle, its wings broken, is at the bottom of the pit.

Now it is the eagle's turn to pray to Shamash, which he does every day. Eventually Shamash responds:

> 'You are wicked, and you have grieved my heart.
> You did an unforgivable deed, an abomination to the gods.
> You are dying, and I shall not go near you!
> But a man, whom I am sending to you, is coming – let him help you.'

The man is Etana, who has also been praying every day to Shamash:

> 'O Lord, let the word go forth from your mouth
> And give me the plant of birth,
> Show me the plant of birth!
> Remove my shame and provide me with a son!'

Shamash gives Etana precise instructions where to find the abandoned eagle, telling him that the bird will then show him the plant of birth.

Tablet III begins with Etana finding the eagle in the pit and asking the bird to show him the plant of birth. The eagle readily agrees, but first must be helped out of the pit; and so with great patience, Etana teaches the eagle to fly again. One month, two months, three, four, five, six, seven months pass:

> In the eighth month he helped it out of its pit.
> The eagle, now well fed, was as strong as a fierce lion.
> The eagle made its voice heard and spoke to Etana,
> 'My friend, we really are friends, you and I!
> Tell me what you wish from me, that I may give it to you.'

Etana wastes no time in asking the eagle to change his destiny, to find
the plant of birth. The eagle hunts around in the mountains but cannot find
the plant, so then suggests to Etana that it carry him upwards on its back:

> 'Put your arms over my sides,
> Put your hands over the quills of my wings.'

Etana puts his arms over the eagle's sides, and his hands over the quills of
its wings and they soar upwards for one mile. The eagle says to Etana: 'My
friend, look at the country! How does it seem?' Etana replies that the wide
sea is no bigger than a sheepfold. Up they go a second mile:

> 'My friend, look at the country! How does it seem?'
> 'The country has turned into a garden . . .
> And the wide sea is no bigger than a bucket!'

A third mile they soar and the eagle asks again. But this time Etana replies
that he cannot even see the country, nor pick out the wide sea.

> 'My friend, I cannot go any further towards heaven.
> Retrace the way, and let me go back to my city!'

The eagle takes him back to earth, and there follows a gap of uncertain length
in which apparently they return to Kish and Etana has a series of dreams
encouraging him to try again to reach heaven. The eagle takes him up once
more – one mile, two miles, a third – and they arrive at the heaven of Anu.
The eagle and Etana pass through the gate of Sin, Shamash, Adad and Ishtar;
they bow down, and there the text breaks off. We do not know what happened
in the heaven of Anu, but we may perhaps guess that at some stage they
did find the plant of birth for at least in the Sumerian king-list, Etana is
succeeded by a son named Balih.

Adapa

Adapa, like Etana and Gilgamesh, is a mortal of divine extraction and, like
Gilgamesh, he narrowly misses immortality but receives compensation – in
his case, becoming the wisest of men.

Adapa is a priest of Ea in his cult temple at Eridu. Every day Adapa
attends to the rites: he bakes bread and sets up offering tables and, as temple
fisherman, he goes out in his boat to catch fish. One day his regimented
routine is disrupted by South Wind, though we do not know exactly how,
since there is a gap of uncertain length. When the text resumes, Adapa is
berating South Wind and threatening to break its wing. He then does this
and, for seven days, South Wind does not blow towards the land. Anu notices
and asks his vizier Ilabrat the reason. Ilabrat tells him that Adapa has broken
South Wind's wing, and Anu demands Adapa's presence. Before Adapa sets
off, however, Ea warns him:

> 'When you stand before Anu
> They will hold out for you bread of death, so you must not eat.
> They will hold out for you water of death, so you must not drink.'

Adapa arrives before Anu and explains what has happened:

> 'My lord, I was catching fish in the middle of the sea
> For the house of my lord [Ea].
> But he inflated the sea into a storm
> And South Wind blew and sank me!
> I was forced to take up residence in the fishes' home
> In my fury I cursed South Wind.'

Dumuzi and Gizzida, two door-keeper gods, speak a word in Adapa's favour to Anu. This calms him down, and he instructs food and drink to be given to Adapa.

> They fetched him the bread of [eternal] life, but he would not eat.
> They fetched him the water of [eternal] life, but he would not drink.

Adapa, remembering Ea's instructions, has rejected the bread and water of immortality. Unfortunately the rest of the epic is lost; we do not know if Ea deliberately tricked Adapa, or whether Ea genuinely believed that Adapa would be offered the bread and water of death.

The Epic of Anzu

With this epic we return to the theme, familiar from the Epic of Creation, of a rebellious contender for supreme power who resorts to trickery and cheating to achieve his ends, whereupon a saviour must be found to defeat

Drawing of a relief from the palace of Ninurta at Nimrud. Ninurta attacks the wicked bird Anzu.

the usurper in heroic combat. In this case we have the evil Anzu, the soaring, bird-shaped son of Anu.

The epic again begins with the formula 'I sing of ...' In the Standard version the hero is the war-god Ninurta. In the Old Babylonian version, the hero is Ningirsu, patron god of the city of Girsu in central Mesopotamia; this version is written in an abbreviated form, and we have only a small part of it.

The story begins with a prologue introducing Ninurta and telling of his powerful feats. Then the gods report to Ellil the birth of Anzu; the full description of him is very fragmentary, but what there is suggests strength, power and fury. At first Ea persuades Ellil to let Anzu serve him as his personal bodyguard, and Ellil appoints Anzu to guard the entrance to his chamber. In Anzu's presence, Ellil often bathes in holy water. Anzu looks on longingly:

> His eyes would gaze at the trappings of Ellil-power:
> His lordly crown, his robe of divinity,
> The Tablet of Destinies in his hands. Anzu gazed,
> And gazed at Duranki's god, father of the gods,
> And fixed his purpose, to usurp the Ellil-power.

Very soon, his wicked plan is made.

> And at the chamber's entrance from which he often gazed, he waited for the start
>   of day.
> When Ellil was bathing in the holy water,
> Stripped and with his crown laid down on the throne,
> He gained the Tablet of Destinies for himself,
> Took away the Ellil-power.

Anzu flies off into hiding with the divine regalia, and Anu immediately calls for Anzu's assassination. First he calls upon his own son Adad to strike Anzu with lightning, his weapon, promising him supremacy in the gods' assembly if he succeeds. But Adad will not go:

> 'Father, who could rush off to the inaccessible mountain?
> Which of the gods your sons will be Anzu's conqueror?
> For he has gained the Tablet of Destinies for himself,
> Has taken away the Ellil-power; rites are abandoned!'

He turns away, saying he will not undertake the expedition. Next, the gods summon Gerra to burn Anzu with fire, his weapon. Gerra replies:

> 'Father, who could rush off to the inaccessible mountain?
> Which of the gods your sons will be Anzu's conqueror?
> For he has gained the Tablet of Destinies for himself,
> Has taken away the Ellil-power; rites are abandoned!'

He also turns away, saying he will not undertake the expedition.

Next they call upon Shara, Ishtar's son to strike (?) Anzu with ..., his weapon (quite what this is we do not know, as the text is broken here). But Shara, too, rejects the chance for glory in identical words. At the third rejection, the gods fall silent, and despair.

Ea, 'the Lord of intelligence', then forms an idea in the depths of his being. He summons Belet-ili, the great mother goddess, to produce broad-chested Ninurta, her 'superb beloved'. This she does, and she makes an inspiring appeal:

'Make a path, fix the hour,
Let light dawn for the gods whom I created.
Muster your devastating battle force,
Make your evil winds flash as they march over him.
Capture soaring Anzu
And inundate the earth, which I created – wreck his dwelling.
Let terror thunder above him,
Let fear your battle force shake in him,
Make the devastating whirlwind rise up against him.
Set your arrow in the bow, coat it with poison'.

Thus inspired, Ninurta marshals the seven evil winds 'who dance in the dust'. He musters a terrifying battle array.

On the mountainside Anzu and Ninurta met.
Anzu looked at him and shook with rage at him,
Bared his teeth like an *ūmu*-demon; his mantle of radiance covered the mountain,
He roared like a lion in sudden rage . . .

A furious battle ensues:

Clouds of death rained down, an arrow flashed lightning,
Whizzed, the battle force roared between them.

Ninurta draws his bow taut and sends another arrow, but Anzu, holding the Tablet of Destinies, easily deflects it. Ninurta sends for advice to Ea. Ea tells the messenger:

'Don't let the battle slacken, press home your victory!
Tire him out so that he sneds his pinions in the clash of tempests.
Take a throw-stick to follow your arrows
And cut off his pinions, detach both right and left . . .'

The messenger returns to Ninurta and repeats Ea's advice word for word. Ninurta marshals once more his seven evil winds and enters the fray again.

At this exciting moment, Tablet II ends. The beginning of Tablet III is very fragmentary, but it seems that devastation reigns; there is blazing heat and confusion during which Ninurta's arrow passes through the heart and lungs of Anzu and he slays the wicked bird. Ninurta regains the Tablet of Destinies and sends the good news winging back to the gods. The epic ends in traditional fashion:

'You captured Anzu, slew him in his powerfulness,
Slew soaring Anzu in his powerfulness.
Because you were so brave and slew the mountain,
You made all foes kneel at the feet of Ellil your father.
Ninurta, because you were so brave and slew the mountain,
You made all foes kneel at the feet of Ellil your father.
You have won complete dominion, every single rite.'

Cylinder seal impression (above) showing Ninurta with his bow
and arrow dispatching the Anzu bird.

Terracotta figure (right) of a nude goddess. The bird feet and
hanging wings suggest the Queen of the Underworld.

The gods then call him by some twenty honorific names, just as Marduk
was named at the end of the Epic of Creation.

The Descent of Ishtar to the Underworld

Unfortunately incomplete, this is a most elegant tale of how (but not why)
the goddess Ishtar descended to the underworld, Kurnugi, the land of no
return, and how, once there, she was imprisoned until Ea secured her release.
The underworld is a dark, dismal and horribly dusty place where Ishtar's
sister Ereshkigal is queen.

Ishtar arrives at the gate of Kurnugi, determined to enter.

> 'Here gatekeeper, open your gate for me,
> Open your gate for me to come in!
> If you do not open the gate for me to come in,
> I shall smash the door and shatter the bolt,
> I shall smash the doorpost and overturn the doors,
> I shall raise up the dead and they shall eat the living:
> The dead shall outnumber the living!'

The gatekeeper goes at once to Ereshkigal:

> When Ereshkigal heard this,
> Her face grew livid as cut tamarisk,
> Her lips grew dark as the rim of a *kuninu*-vessel.*
> *The rim of a kuninu-vessel was coated with bitumen, making it black-lipped*

She asks herself what can have brought Ishtar to her kingdom, and ominously
instructs the gatekeeper:

'Go, gatekeeper, open your gate to her.
Treat her according to the ancient rites.'

There follows a ritualistic and repetitive scene in seven stages, typical of Mesopotamian myth, in which the beautiful and gorgeously attired Ishtar is systematically stripped of her jewellery. At the first gate, Ishtar is stripped of the great crown on her head.

'Gatekeeper, why have you taken away the great crown on my head?'
'Go in, my lady. Such are the rites of the Mistress of Earth.'

At the second gate, Ishtar is stripped of the rings in her ears.

'Gatekeeper, why have you taken away the rings in my ears?'
'Go in, my lady. Such are the rites of the Mistress of Earth.'

At the third gate, Ishtar is stripped of the beads around her neck; at the fourth of the toggle-pins at her breast; at the fifth of the girdle of birth-stones around her waist; at the sixth of the bangles on her wrists and ankles; and at the seventh gate she is stripped of the proud garment of her body. Thus she is naked when she finally comes before her sister, but still it is Ereshkigal who trembles. The queen of the underworld summons her vizier Namtar and instructs him to send out against Ishtar sixty diseases – to her eyes, her arms, her feet, her heart, her head, to every part of her.

Meanwhile, on earth, all sexual activity is at an end.

No bull mounted a cow, no donkey impregnated a jenny,
No young man impregnated a girl in the street,
The young man slept in his private room,
The girl slept in the company of her friends.

Papsukkal, the vizier of the great gods, weeps before Ea, and Ea as usual comes up with a solution. He creates a playboy whose beauty will so gladden Ereshkigal's heart that she will relax; 'her mood will lighten'. He must then ask for a waterskin, possibly under the pretence of drinking from it, and sprinkle Ishtar with its contents so that she may revive.

This ruse fails, however. Initially charmed with his appearance, Ereshkigal suddenly curses him with a great curse:

'Bread gleaned from the city's ploughs shall be your food,
The city drains shall be your only drinking place,
The shade of a city wall your only standing place,
Threshold steps your only sitting place,
The drunkard and the thirsty shall slap your cheek.'

But, in cursing Ea's playboy, she spares Ishtar. She instructs Namtar to sprinkle her with the waters of life and, in a highly satisfactory symmetrical passage reversing her earlier progress, Ishtar is let out of each of the seven gates by which she entered; at each one she repossesses, in strict sequence, the symbols of her divinity, starting with the proud garment of her body and ending with the great crown for her head.

The epic ends with Ishtar paying for her release with Dumuzi, 'the lover

Cylinder seal impression which may portray Dumuzi retained in the underworld, flanked by snakes.

of her youth', who will in future dwell in the underworld. On one day each year he will return to earth at which time rituals will be enacted. This probably refers to the *taklimtu* ritual which took place in the month of Dumuzi (June/July), during which a statue of Dumuzi was bathed, anointed and lay in state in Nineveh.

Nergal and Ereshkigal

This is a myth which has a considerable overlap with Ishtar's Descent to the Underworld, sharing some of the same characters, the same location, and Ea's role in bringing about a solution. As we shall see, there are interesting differences, however, such as the introduction of a ritual chair, the graphic image of a long stairway leading up to and down from the heaven of the gods, and the fact that it is a god, Nergal, who makes the descent and becomes Ereshkigal's husband.

The myth begins with Anu deciding that, since it is impossible for Ereshkigal to come up to them for their annual banquet, or for them to go down to her, her messenger must come to the table and take her portion down to her. Anu sends Kakka, his messenger, to tell Ereshkigal. Kakka goes down the long stairway of heaven, and this time the gatekeeper is welcoming: 'Kakka, come in, and may the gate bless you.'

Seven gates there are, but Kakka is divested of nothing as he passes through them. After the seventh gate Kakka finds himself in Ereshkigal's presence; kneeling down, he kisses the ground in front of her and reports verbatim Anu's message. Ereshkigal and Kakka then exchange pleasantries, and she decides to send her vizier Namtar to fetch her portion.

Unfortunately, the text is somewhat fragmentary at the point when Namtar arrives before the great gods, but it would appear that the god Nergal insults Namtar and is sent by Ea to Ereshkigal. Nergal, however, first equips himself with a special chair which may have had a ritualistic role in warding off evil spirits. He is also forewarned by Ea with the usual cautionary advice: not to sit on any chair they might bring, not to eat bread or meat, not to drink beer, not to wash his feet, and certainly not to succumb to Ereshkigal's charms after she

> '... has been to the bath,
> And dressed herself in a fine dress,
> Allowing you to glimpse her body.'

Nergal then sets his face towards Kurnugi, which is described exactly as it was in Ishtar's Descent. When he arrives he is made to wait by the gatekeeper, who goes to Ereshkigal to report his arrival. Meanwhile the vizier Namtar sees Nergal standing in the shadow of the gate.

> Namtar's face went as livid as cut tamarisk.
> His lips grew dark as the rim of a *kuninu*-vessel.

Namtar tells Ereshkigal of the insult, but she is scornful and tells Namtar to bring Nergal to her. Through seven gates, each with a name, Nergal passes and after the seventh, the gate of Ennugigi, he enters the broad courtyard. There he kneels down, kisses the ground in front of Ereshkigal, and explains that Anu has sent him. They bring him a chair; he will not sit on it. The baker brings him bread; he will not eat it. The butcher brings him meat; he will not eat it. The brewer brings him beer; he will not drink it. They bring him a footbath; he will not wash his feet.

Ereshkigal goes to the bath, dresses herself in fine dress, allowing him to catch a glimpse of her body and 'He resisted his heart's desire to do what men and women do'. Unfortunately his resistance is short-lived; after a short break, Ereshkigal again goes to the bath, again dresses herself in a fine dress and again allows him to catch a glimpse of her body. This time, 'He gave in to his heart's desire to do what men and women do'.

Abandoning all restraint, Ereshkigal and Nergal spend a first and second day, a third and fourth day, a fifth and sixth day, passionately in bed together. When the seventh day comes, Nergal says he must leave and he ascends the long stairway of heaven to stand before Anu, Ellil and Ea.

Meanwhile, in Kurnugi, tears are flowing down Ereshkigal's cheeks:

> 'Erra [Nergal] the lover of my delight –
> I did not have enough delight with him before he left!'

Namtar offers to go to Anu, there to 'arrest' Nergal so that he may kiss her again. Ereshkigal agrees:

> 'Go, Namtar, you must speak to Anu, Ellil, and Ea!
> Set your face towards the gate of Anu, Ellil, and Ea,
> To say, ever since I was a child and a daughter,

I have not known the playing of other girls,
I have not known the romping of children.
The god whom you sent to me and who has impregnated me – let him sleep with
    me again!
Send that god to us, and let him spend the night with me as my lover!'

She threatens that if he is not sent back to her, she will raise up the dead
so that they outnumber the living – the identical threat made by Ishtar in
Kurnugi, and by Ishtar to her father in the Epic of Gilgamesh when she wants
the Bull of Heaven.

Namtar ascends the long stairway of heaven and repeats Ereshkigal's
speech verbatim, including her threat. Ea then arranges an identity parade
of the gods so that Namtar may search out the wrong-doer, but Namtar
does not recognise the recreant. He returns to Ereshkigal and tells her that,
in the assembly of the gods, there was one 'who sat bareheaded, blinking
and cringing'. She instantly tells him to return and fetch that god.

In a somewhat fragmentary passage, Nergal is at last identified and,
armed with his magic chair, descends once more the long stairway of heaven.
He does not wait for the seven gates to be opened: he strikes down Nedu,
the doorman of the first gate, the second doorman, the third, fourth, fifth,
sixth and seventh. Entering the wide courtyard, he goes up to Ereshkigal
and laughs, and pulls her by her hair from the throne.

Passionately they go to bed, again for a first and second day, a third
and fourth, a fifth and a sixth. When the seventh day arrives the text breaks
off, and we do not know exactly what happens in the end. But there is a
much shorter and earlier version of the same text (called the Amarna Version
since is was found at Tell el-Amarna in Egypt), which ends with Ereshkigal
saying to Nergal, after she has been unceremoniously pulled from her throne:

'You can be my husband, and I can be your wife.
I will let you seize
Kingship over the wide Earth! I will put the tablet
Of wisdom in your hand! You can be master,
I can be mistress.' Nergal listened to this speech of hers,
And seized her and kissed her. He wiped away her tears.
'What have you asked of me? After so many months,
It shall certainly be so!'

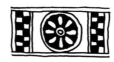

Myth and meaning

Myths can be interpreted in a variety of ways: they can portray cosmic forces personified, as for example when chaos is subdued by order; they can reflect historical events such as military campaigns, the building of city walls and the return of cult statues; they can serve purely cultic purposes, for example, for recitation at the New Year's Festival; and events in them can mirror the cycle of nature, thus reassuring their audience that the national gods are in control. All these interpretations are possible when we consider Mesopotamian myths. We can also identify recurrent themes, such as combat with impossibly over-sized opponents or against hopeless odds, the quest for immortality or eternal youth, and the journey to the underworld. Heroes of myth share universal characteristics: bravery, honour, fidelity and beauty. They often have miraculous births, or divine mothers and/or fathers. The way in which a myth impresses itself upon the community does not differ very much from one civilisation to another, and the myths of Mesopotamia bear hallmarks familiar from other languages and other times.

But in one way they are exceptional. The myths described in this book are among the earliest ever formulated and recorded. Their origins are lost in the sands of time but probably lie as far back as the building of the first cities during the fourth to the third millennium BC, when the features of gods were attributed to real kings and the prestige of particular gods was deliberately enhanced in order to honour cult centres and thereby their inhabitants.

The far-ranging sweep of subject, character and location in these myths makes a strong appeal across the millennia that divide them from their modern audience. We in the West may be so steeped in the literary and religious traditions stemming from classical Greece and the Bible that, from our late and inescapably sophisticated viewpoint, we may be tempted to ascribe to them qualities they did not have for the ancient Mesopotamians. Simply to comprehend a polytheistic viewpoint may be beyond us, and it is also vital to bear in mind that our knowledge is incomplete – we have what may well be only a small number of the pieces in a large jigsaw, with no concept of the overall design. And we must also remember that these tablets were never intended for us to read.

Nevertheless, close study reveals characteristics and patterns which may help us reach more deeply to the heart of these myths. We have seen how the pace of action is always stately and slow-moving, how a change of location

Two winged bulls flanking the main entrance to the throne room of the palace of Sargon II (722–705 BC) at Khorsabad: in their original state (below), and the artist's reconstruction (above).

Ivory mirror handle from Enkomi in Cyprus, about 1200–1100 BC. It shows the climax of a cosmic battle.

*Limestone plaque surmounted with the head
of a demon, used to expel evil spirits, a
number of which appear on the other side.
The top register portrays symbols of heavenly
gods, and demons threaten the sick man in
the third register. Hell lies beneath.*

is always effected by the simple expedient of the hero of the myth actually
going there. There is no 'meanwhile' device to describe what is happening
elsewhere in time or place to other characters involved in the story; only
one narrative can develop at a time. The plot is advanced in various simple
ways: by dreams which presage future events, by conversations between the
main protagonists, by gods giving instructions and advice.

We have seen how repetition is widely used, usually word for word,
with no elegant variations of vocabulary. Reality is reinforced by repetition.
Some passages in the Epic of Creation are repeated *en bloc* as many as four
times, and there is not a single myth which does not contain such repetition.
Sometimes this is used to heighten dramatic tension, as for example when

Sculptured relief of a powerful Gilgamesh-type hero carrying a lion cub. From the palace of Sargon II at Khorsabad.

the eagle takes Etana up to the heaven of Anu, or when Gilgamesh is making his way through the dark wasteland. It also serves to emphasise the importance of certain descriptive passages and to encourage an audience unused to visual images to use its mind's eye to see what mattered and exactly what was at stake for the heroes engaged in the action. Thus, when Tiamat's gang of demons is described over and over again, the audience was meant to see and feel exactly how terrifying and formidable they were. That is the stuff of which story-telling is made.

Another epic device is to reach a number and then crown it by moving on just one higher. Thus there is the crowning of six days by the seventh after the great Flood, when the mountain Nimush held the boat fast:

Romantic view, published in the early eighteenth century, of the ruins of Persepolis.

> The first and second day the mountain Nimush held the boat fast and did not let
>   it budge.
> The third and fourth day the mountain Nimush held the boat fast and did not
>   let it budge.
> The fifth and sixth day the mountain Nimush held the boat fast and did not let
>   it budge.
> When the seventh day arrived . . .

So also Gilgamesh falls into a deep sleep which lasts six days and six nights. On the seventh day he wakes up. Nergal and Ereshkigal lie passionately in bed for six days and six nights. On the seventh day, real life resumes. In the Epic of Creation, two gods are sent to overcome Tiamat. They fail, and it is the third, Marduk, who succeeds. In the Epic of Anzu, three gods try and fail, and the fourth, Ninurta, succeeds. Numbers are generally significant, particularly three and seven. Dreams tend to come in threes, and winds and weapons in sevens. Tension is increased by cumulative effect.

To attempt to assess the literary merit of these texts is doubtless to undertake a perilous task in which there are endless opportunities for error. The various literary devices must reflect the taste of the original audience, an audience whose tastes lay not so much in nail-biting drama but more in sophisticated complexity and moral purpose. Gods played a far greater part in the life of the ancient world than can easily be comprehended today, when it seems there are scientific explanations for everything. However we ourselves try to evaluate the appeal of these texts, on whatever grounds – their purpose, style or content – we have to realise our own limitations. Perhaps we should let simple enjoyment – of glorious Gilgamesh, ravishing jewel-hung Ishtar, evil Anzu, proud Marduk, wise Ea, shaggy Enkidu, mysterious Utnapishtim, black-lipped Ereshkigal – be the strongest factor. In the end, the art of recounting myths has one purpose only: to fire the imagination of those who listen or read. The fires of Mesopotamian myth still burn bright.

Suggestions for further reading

Although Akkadian as a written language died out in the first century AD, our modern understanding of it continues to progress. The great Assyrian dictionary produced by the Oriental Institute of the University of Chicago is still being published, and each new volume inevitably generates some new interpretations of and ideas concerning the detail of ancient texts, even if the general sense of the whole seldom requires alteration. The most recent work on the whole corpus, already referred to in the introduction, is *Myths from Mesopotamia* by Stephanie Dalley (Oxford, 1989). Other new research on the Epic of Gilgamesh, including some hitherto unpublished fragments, is being done by Andrew George and will be published under the title *The Babylonian Gilgamesh Epic* in 1993 by the Oxford University Press. For a highly technical discussion of the epic, *The Evolution of the Gilgamesh Epic* by J. H. Tigay (Philadelphia, 1982) is probably the best. *Atra-hasis: The Babylonian Story of the Flood* by W. G. Lambert and A. R. Millard (Oxford, 1969) is the standard work on the full text of this myth.

For an overview of Mesopotamian texts as a whole, and indeed for comparisons with other ancient texts, look at *Ancient Near Eastern Texts*, edited by James B. Pritchard (Princeton, 1969). Apart from myths, epics and legends, it includes sections on legal and historical texts, rituals, incantations and descriptions of festivals, hymns and prayers, didactic and wisdom literature, lamentations, letters, sacred marriage texts and love songs.

There are many books about the history and civilization of Assyria and Babylonia, among which I would draw attention to *Ancient Mesopotamia* by A. L. Oppenheim (Chicago, 1977), *Babylon* by J. Oates (London, 1986) and *The Might That Was Assyria* by H. W. F. Saggs (London, 1984). The first and second works mentioned have been revised and updated, and all three provide useful background information.

On the rediscovery of this ancient land, Seton Lloyd has recently revised and enlarged his fascinating and well-illustrated book *Foundations in the Dust* (London, 1980). An excellent general picture of the rediscovery of many ancient civilisations is provided by H. V. F. Winstone in *Uncovering the Ancient World* (London, 1985). For the cuneiform script itself, Christopher Walker of the Department of Western Asiatic Antiquities in the British Museum has given a thorough survey, including some sample texts, in *Cuneiform* (*Reading the Past* series, London, 1987).

On the general subject of myth, there are of course many hundreds of books and articles which are worth consulting. In the Near Eastern context, I would recommend G. S. Kirk's *Myth: Its Meaning and Functions in Ancient and Other Cultures* (Cambridge, 1971) and, to a lesser extent, *Middle Eastern Mythology* by S. H. Hooke, published by Penguin Books (1963).

Index and picture credits

Picture credits

Front cover: Musée du Louvre, Paris, AO 19826; *pp. 4–5:* D. Collon; *p. 10: (left)* W. Blunt, *Pietro's Pilgrimage,* London 1953; *(right)* British Museum; *p. 11: (left)* E. Flandin and P. Coste, *Voyage en Perse,* Paris 1851; *(right)* BM WA 118885; *p. 12: (top)* BM MLA 1976. 9–3. 1; *(bottom)* BM MLA 1987. 3-2. 1; *p. 13: (left)* BM; *(right)* BM MLA 1987. 1–9. 1; *p. 15: (left)* BM; *(right)* E.A. Wallis Budge, *Rise and Progress of Assyriology,* London 1925; *p. 20:* BM WA K3375; *p. 21: (left)* BM WA 124867; *(right)* M.E.L. Mallowan, *Nimrud and its Remains,* London 1966; *p. 23:* BM WA 118822; *p. 26:* E. Unger, *Babylon: die heilige Stadt nach der Beschreibung der Babylonier,* Berlin 1931; *p. 27: (top)* BM WA 89115; *(centre)* BM WA 89110; *(bottom)* BM WA 132257; *p. 28: (top)* Iraq Museum, Baghdad, IM 15218; *(bottom)* BM WA 89311; *p. 30: (top)* G. Loud, *The Megiddo Ivories,* Chicago 1939, pl. 4; *(bottom)* The Pierpont Morgan Library, New York, 653; *p. 31: (top)* BM WA 124543; *(bottom)* BM WA 102416; *p. 32:* BM WA 124655; *p. 33:* P. Thureau-Dangin and M. Dunand, *Til-Barsip,* Paris 1936; *p. 34:* BM WA 78260; *p. 39:* E. Ebeling and B. Meissner, *Reallexicon der Assyriologie,* Berlin 1928; *p. 41:* BM WA 116624; *p. 42:* BM WA 103226; *p. 44:* BM WA 89435; *p. 46:* M. von Oppenheim, *Tell Halaf: A New Culture in Oldest Mesopotamia,* London and New York 1933; *p. 50:* G. Contenau, *Manuel d'Archeologie Orientale,* vol. II, Paris 1931; *p. 53: (top)* BM WA 118932; *(bottom)* BM WA 122125; *p. 54: (top)* BM WA 22961; *(bottom)* The Oriental Institute of The University of Chicago, A 18161; *p. 57:* Babylon/D. Collon; *p. 58:* Unger *(ibid);* *p. 61:* Ur 18122; *p. 63:* BM WA 129480; *p. 66:* D. Bell-Scott, from H. Frankfort, *The Art and Architecture of the Ancient Orient,* London 1954; *p. 69: (left)* The Pierpont Morgan Library, 689; *(right)* BM WA 103226; *p. 71:* BM WA 123279; *p. 75: (top)* P.E. Botta and E. Flandin, *Monuments de Nineve,* Paris 1849–50; *(bottom)* BM GR 1897. 4–1. 872; *p. 76:* Ebeling and Meissner *(ibid);* *p. 77:* Botta and Flandin *(ibid);* *p. 78:* C. De Bruin, *Travels into Muscovy, Persia and part of the East Indies,* London 1737.